RAJASTHAN

POCKET GUIDE

Walking Eye
mobile app

Discover the world's best destinations with the Insight Guides Walking Eye app, available to download for free in the App Store and Google Play.

The container app provides easy access to fantastic free content on events and activities taking place in your current location or chosen destination, with the possibility of booking, as well as the regularly-updated Insight Guides travel blog: Inspire Me. In addition, you can purchase curated, premium destination guides through the app, which feature local highlights, hotel, bar, restaurant and shopping listings, an A to Z of practical information and more. Or purchase and download Insight Guides eBooks straight to your device.

TOP 10 ATTRACTIONS

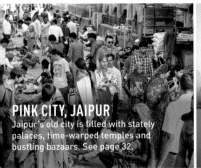

PINK CITY, JAIPUR
Jaipur's old city is filled with stately palaces, time-warped temples and bustling bazaars. See page 32.

UDAIPUR
Fairy-tale palaces and havelis clustered around Lake Pichola. See page 77.

RANTHAMBORE NATIONAL PARK
This is one of the best places on the planet to see wild tigers in their natural environment. See page 47.

PUSHKAR CAMEL FAIR
The peaceful town of Pushkar sees a spectacular annual camel fair. See page 60.

RANAKPUR TEMPLES
Exquisite cluster of Jain temples hidden deep in the wooded hills of southern Rajasthan. See page 84.

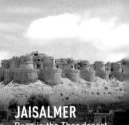

JAISALMER
Deep in the Thar desert, this citadel is a magical sight. See page 73.

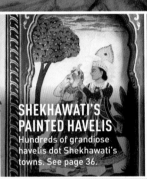

SHEKHAWATI'S PAINTED HAVELIS
Hundreds of grandiose havelis dot Shekhawati's towns. See page 36.

CHITTAURGARH FORT
The rugged fort of Chittaurgarh saw some of the most celebrated and most terrible events in Rajasthan's history. See page 53.

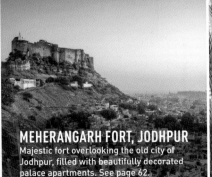

MEHERANGARH FORT, JODHPUR
Majestic fort overlooking the old city of Jodhpur, filled with beautifully decorated palace apartments. See page 62.

BUNDI
Home to a remarkable collection of traditional paintings. See page 50.

A PERFECT TOUR

Day 1

Jaipur

Start in Jaipur, which is easily reached from Delhi by express train. Spend a day in the Pink City, exploring the magnificent City Palace, Hawa Mahal and Jantar Mantar in the morning, followed by an afternoon exploring the city's marvellous bazaars.

Days 5 and 6

Jaisalmer

Take the train to Jaisalmer and spend a day exploring the magical desert citadel of Jaisalmer, followed by a camel trek into the sands.

Days 3 and 4

Jodhpur

Continue to Jodhpur and spend time exploring the city's majestic Meherangarh Fort and the fascinating back alleys and busy bazaars of its historic old city.

Days 2 and 3

Pushkar

Take the train to Ajmer then hop in a bus or taxi to reach the nearby temple town of Pushkar, one of Rajasthan's most idyllic destinations. If you have time, it's well worth exploring Ajmer itself and its vibrant shrine to the great Sufi saint Muin-ud-din Chishti.

OF **RAJASTHAN**

Days 7 to 9

Udaipur

From here, you'll need to retrace your steps to Jodhpur (where you might prefer to break your journey overnight), then head down to southern Rajasthan and the picture-perfect lakeside city of Udaipur. The sprawling fort at Kumbulgarh and the exquisite Jain temples of Rankapur can also be visited in a day-trip from the city.

Day 10

Chittaurgarh

From Udaipur, it's a relatively short journey east to the vast hilltop fort of Chittaurgarh, for centuries the most powerful city in Rajasthan, now hauntingly deserted.

Days 11 and 12

Bundi

Another relatively short journey east brings you to Bundi, home to one of the state's smaller but most beautiful palaces and a great place to rest and recharge.

Days 13 and 14

Ranthambore

Continue north to Ranthambore and end your tour with a tiger safari in the world-famous Ranthambore National Park. From here, it's a straightforward train journey back to Jaipur, and on to Delhi.

CONTENTS

🔘 **FEATURES**

INTRODUCTION

Rajasthan is India at its most Indian: a dazzling kaleidoscope of colour and culture, and a feast for the senses and the imagination. Rugged citadels and fortresses dot the arid landscape, concealing exquisitely decorated palaces and temples within. Bazaars overflow with gorgeously tie-dyed and embroidered textiles, patrolled by crowds of extravagantly turbaned men and jewellery-laden women in glittering saris. Regal opulence, religious fervour and consummate craftsmanship characterize the towns and cities, while strutting camels and prowling tigers roam the state's forests and dunes. All of which adds up to one of the world's most beguiling travel destinations, offering glimpses of a place into which the modern world often seems barely to intrude.

◎ THE RAJPUTS

Exactly who the Rajputs are and where they originally came from remains something of a mystery. Some claim they were of Indian, others of foreign, descent, although the truth is probably a mix of the two. Whoever they were, the Rajputs were to dominate the history of the region for centuries to come, and provided Rajasthan with most of its leading ruling families. Never exceeding seven or eight percent of Rajasthan's total population, the Rajputs remained the ruling class *par excellence* for centuries, segregating themselves from the rest of society by their social status, military prowess and code of honour. The name 'Rajput' itself derives from a corruption of *rajputras*, sons of princes, hence the region's traditional name of Rajputana, the land of the rajas, subsequently modified to Rajasthan.

Rajasthan is, above all, a land of contrasts. Large parts of the state are arid semi-desert; a sere, sand-covered expanse against which the region's vibrantly dressed inhabitants stand out all the more vividly. Colour saturates every surface, as if to compensate for the monochrome landscape, from the Pink City of Jaipur and the pale blue streets of Jodhpur, through to the honey-coloured havelis (traditional mansions) of Jaisalmer and the snowy-white palaces of Udaipur. Delicate apartments of marble and mirrorwork sit hidden behind forbidding fortifications, silent witnesses to some of the subcontinent's bloodiest battles. Palaces of fabulous opulence and extravagance provide a living memento of the days of the all-powerful Rajput maharajas, while mud-walled villages dot the desert, lit by fires of animal dung.

Two Rajputs warriors

Historically, too, Rajasthan is a land of extremes, long-dominated by the chivalric Rajput clans, whose all-encompassing code of military honour led its menfolk to repeated acts of suicidal bravery while their women, preferring death to dishonour, cast themselves into the flames of mass funeral pyres. In more recent centuries the state's gilded maharajas led lives of astonishing opulence, even whilst their subjects subsisted in the most grinding poverty.

Thar desert

LIE OF THE LAND

Sprawling across the margins of northwestern India, Rajasthan is bounded by Pakistan to the west and the states of Gujarat and Madhya Pradesh to the south and southeast. The scale of Rajasthan should not be underestimated. The largest state in the world's seventh biggest country, the region covers an area almost the size of Germany, with all the major cities separated from one another by sizeable journeys by road or rail.

Geographically, Rajasthan comprises two distinct regions divided by the Aravalli Mountains, which run southwest to northeast across the state. The western and northern parts of the state (including the areas around Jodhpur, Jaisalmer and Bikaner) are predominantly arid semi-desert, merging in the west of the state with the great Thar Desert, which straddles the border with Pakistan. The other side of the Aravalli divide is significantly less arid, while parts of southern and southwestern Rajasthan are unexpectedly verdant, boasting areas of dense forest and fertile irrigated valleys that support the historic cities of Udaipur, Kota and Chittorgarh. The state capital of Jaipur sits in the shadow of the Aravallis, more or less at the junction between these two contrasting climatic and geographical zones.

Much of the state's population of 70 million people is concentrated in the major cities, densest in the east of the state but thinning dramatically as one heads west into the deepest and barely inhabited reaches of the Thar Desert. The winter months (roughly November to February) are the best time to visit, with a pleasantly temperate Mediterranean climate and daytime temperatures around 25°C (77°F). The temperature begins to rise in March and April, peaking at around 36°C (97°F) during May and June, before the arrival of the monsoon from July to September cools things down again. Things becoming increasingly arid as you head west, while the desert regions around Jaisalmer and Bikaner offer typical climactic extremes, punishingly hot by day, but sometimes unexpectedly chilly by night.

RAJASTHAN URBAN AND PASTORAL

Cultural contrasts are similarly marked, ranging from the cosmopolitan coffee houses of Jaipur, catering to a westernized urban elite, to remote desert villages where the daily life still follows an almost medieval pattern, with villagers walking miles daily to collect precious firewood or drinkable water.

It's in the great cities that much of Rajasthan's appeal still lies. Almost all follow a similar pattern, centred on the vast forts from which the state's former rulers exercised military and political power in turbulent times. Dauntingly severe from the outside, these forts conceal luxuriously appointed and extravagantly decorated palaces within showcasing the Rajasthani craftsmanship at its finest – a surreal

Krishna in Rajasthan

The cult of the blue-skinned, flute-playing Krishna is particularly strong in Rajasthan, with the exploits of the playful young god featuring in temples, paintings and festivals across the state, most notably in the vibrant pilgrimage town of Nathdwara, north of Udaipur.

contrast between military severity and extravagant luxury which is typical of the region.

Outside the forts spread Rajasthan's old medieval cities, home extravagant havelis, incense-cloaked temples and some of India's finest bazaars. Here you'll find the region's magnificent artisanal traditions, handed down from generation to generation over the centuries and still going strong today, with craftspeople producing anything and everything from vividly coloured and gorgeously decorated fabrics through to exquisite silverwork and miniature paintings.

There's also plenty to explore away from the major urban centres. The state's eastern fringes boast two of India's finest wildlife reserves: the world-famous Ranthambore National Park, one of the best places on the planet to spot wild tigers in their natural habitat, and Bharatpur National Park, perhaps the subcontinent's premier birdwatching destination. Camel trekking in the Thar Desert is another enduringly popular tourist draw, with expeditions lasting anything from a day to several weeks, departing from either Jaisalmer or Bikaner, offering the chance to roll slowly across the dunes by day and sleep beneath the stars by night.

 # A BRIEF HISTORY

Occupying the strategic routes between the mountains of central Asia and the fertile plains of the Ganges, the history of Rajasthan has been shaped by an eclectic cast of nomads, traders, mystics and marauding armies. Settled by the disparate clans known as the Rajputs, the region was later contested by the Sultans of Delhi and the great Mughals before becoming a vassal of the Britain's Indian Raj. The great forts dotting the state bear witness to the region's history of courtly chivalry and ceaseless conflict, glorious and gruesome in equal measure, which is every bit as colourful as the bright turbans, brocaded saris and tie-dyed textiles of the people who live here.

PREHISTORY

Human settlement came early to the Indian subcontinent, particularly Rajasthan. One of the world's oldest civilizations, Harappan culture (also known as the Indus Valley Civilization) developed along the valley of the Indus River from around 3300 BC, supporting a population at its peak (2500–1700 BC) of perhaps as many as five million people, spread across dozens of highly developed towns and villages. Most of the major Harappan sites lie in what is now Pakistan, but Rajasthan is home to a small number of Harappan-era sites. These include Kalibangan, in the far northwest of the state, India's largest Harappan settlement and the possible site of the world's oldest ploughed field.

Following the collapse of Harappan civilization, Rajasthan fell for a while to the margins of Indian history, henceforth increasingly centred on the prosperous cities of the fertile Ganges valley to the east.

RAJPUTS AND SULTANS

The 6th and 7th centuries AD saw the major development in Rajasthan's history, with the emergence of a series of powerful new warrior clans. Successive invaders from the west had been steadily settling in Rajasthan from the 3rd century onwards – Shakas (Scythians), Gujaras, Huns and others – or the Rajputs, as they came to be known. As the Rajput clans spread, they divided up much of Rajasthan and beyond amongst themselves. Foremost amongst the early Rajput dynasties were the Chauhans of Ajmer, though several others, most notably the Sisodia rulers of Mewar, with their capital at Chittaurgarh, were also significant.

Muslim invaders from central Asia had also been wandering into India since the year 1000. Muhammad Ghori was the first to venture into Rajput territory, winning a decisive battle against Prithviraj Chauhan of Ajmer in 1192. Ghori's forces subsequently overran much of northwestern India, establishing a new dynasty in Delhi – the Delhi Sultanate – which would survive as the dominant power in the region for over three centuries.

The long years of Sultanate rule were marked by incessant conflict with the Rajputs, with both sides coexisting uneasily over the centuries. Chief scourge of the Rajputs was the fearsome sultan Alauddin Khalji, who reigned from 1296–1316 and conquered many Rajput strongholds, including Chittaurgarh fort in 1303. Seeing the inevitability of defeat, the fort's surviving men rode out to die in battle, while over ten thousand women commited johar by flinging themselves into a vast funeral pyre – scenes that would come to be repeated many times over the following centuries.

Despite intermittent conflicts, the latter years of the Sultanate also saw major developments in Rajasthan. Chittaurgarh itself recovered magnificently following the onslaught of Alauddin under Rana Kumbha, who reigned from 1433–68 and established his Sisodia clan as the pre-eminent force in southern Rajasthan. Meanwhile, the Rathores, based in Jodhpur, emerged as a major power, as did the Kachchwahas of Amber, who would play a particularly crucial role in the next phase of Rajput history.

THE MUGHALS

The long-running Delhi Sultanate was finally ended in 1526 with the arrival of a new wave of Muslim invaders from Central Asia – the Mughals. Mughal power waxed and waned during the rule of the first two emperors, Babur and Humayun, but was firmly consolidated during the reign of the greatest of all Mughal rulers, Akbar, who reigned from 1556–1605.

Avoiding conflict wherever possible, Akbar worked constantly to secure the loyalty of potentially troublesome

Timur, Babur and Humayun

opponents, seeking alliances and granting special privileges to rivals who consented to enter the Mughal fold. Foremost amongst the new clans courted by Akbar were the Rajputs. Akbar began by seeking an alliance with the Kachchwahas of Amber, offering their rulers elevated positions and incomes within the Mughal hierarchy in return for their submission. As a token of friendship Akbar also took a Kachchwaha princess in marriage, the famous Jodha Bai, who became the foremost of his thirty-odd wives and the mother of his successor as Mughal emperor, Jahangir. In addition, Jodha Bai's nephew, Man Singh, subsequently became one of the greatest of all Mughal military commanders, fighting on Akbar's behalf in every corner of the fast-expanding empire, and even leading Mughal forces into battle against his fellow Rajputs.

Encouraged by the early success of his policy, Akbar entered into matrimonial alliances with several other Rajput houses, integrating them into the larger imperial ruling class. The Rajputs, in return, gave the empire their support. By and large, Akbar's policy of rapprochement was enormously successful, with one notable exception: the Sisodia rulers of Chittaurgarh, the most powerful of all the Rajput clans, who remained impervious to

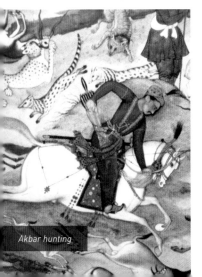

Akbar hunting

Akbar's repeated overtures. Eventually tiring of their defiance, Akbar despatched a huge army south, capturing the city in 1568 after a long and devastating siege lasting almost a year, at the end of which the city's surviving inhabitants were slaughtered. The city was razed, never to recover, and a new Sisodia capital, Udaipur, established at a more remote and easily defensible location.

The birth of a city

Despite waning Rajput power, the 18th century saw one major development in the region's history when the visionary Kachchwaha ruler Jai Singh abandoned his ancestral fort at Amber and established a new city, and future capital of Rajasthan: Jaipur.

The interdependence between the Mughal Empire and the Rajputs lasted for two centuries, until the steep decline in Mughal power during the 18th century led to a similar plunge in Rajput fortunes. The lands of the Rajputs (along with other Mughal territories) were plundered at will by the forces of the increasingly powerful Marathas, from Maharashtra. Several Rajput rulers secured their territories by paying huge sums as an annual ransom – a far cry from the chivalric codes of military honour that had once infused the everyday life of the Rajput ruling class.

THE ARRIVAL OF THE BRITISH

European traders and soldiers had been coming to India since the early 17th century, and were soon sucked into the power vacuum left by the disintegration of the Mughal Empire. Establishing a foothold in Bengal around the mid-18th century, the British – with their advanced firearms and superior military organisation – rapidly made their presence felt across the rest of the country. Aware of the Maratha threat, the British struck a series of treaties with various Rajput states – or the "Princely States" as they would come to be known during the colonial period – obliging each to assist the other in the event of a threat to either side's security. However, such treaties were generally far more advantageous to the British than to the Rajput states.

British military force finally destroyed Maratha ambitions during the Third Anglo-Maratha War of 1817–18, and in doing so, cleared the path to creating an Indian empire of their own. Freed of the Maratha threat, the Rajput states now discovered that they were no longer in a position to deal with the mighty new power on an equal footing. Even so, the British government wisely refrained from depriving any Rajput rulers of their thrones. The wisdom of this policy was later demonstrated when almost all the Rajput princes came rushing to the aid of the beleaguered British during the 1857 Uprising. Rajput loyalty was rewarded with assurances that the princely rulers would be guaranteed their thrones in perpetuity, even as British legal, administrative and educational reforms were bringing the first winds of European change to the region.

A growing nationalist fervour began sweeping India towards the end of the 19th century, starting with the educated Indian elite and gradually trickling down to the masses. Faced by with a growing hostility to foreign rule, the British governor soon realised that the country's privileged rulers might prove important allies in the face of growing popular agitation.

The outbreak of World War I once again saw the rulers in Rajasthan eager to demonstrate their loyalty to Britain, although the character of India's freedom movement began to change considerably after the peace treaty of 1919. While

British imperialism remained the chief target of hostility, attention also began to be directed towards the plight of subjects in the Princely States, throwing the British and the maharajas even more closely into each other's arms. Both parties, however, found themselves ultimately powerless in the face of the independence movement.

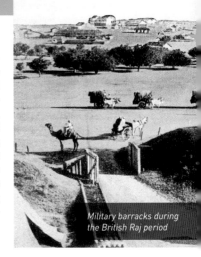

Military barracks during the British Raj period

INDEPENDENT INDIA

India finally achieved independence on 15 August 1947. The rulers of Rajasthan were left in an ambiguous position, technically free of all central control, since their territories had not been formally handed over to the new government of India by the British.

The continued existence of the Princely States within independent India naturally posed a considerable danger to national integrity, already sorely damaged by Partition, and strenuous efforts were made to get the Rajput rulers to merge their territories with the rest of India. Naturally, most of the rulers were reluctant to accept any arrangement that curtailed their power, although they were eventually won over with the promise of various privileges and a generous annual 'privy purse', which they continued to enjoy until Indira Gandhi abolished them in 1970. The new United State of Greater Rajasthan was thus created, although it wasn't until November 1956, when the centrally administered state of Ajmer was added, that the present-day state of Rajasthan finally came into being.

Despite the various sweeteners offered, not surprisingly many of the ex-rulers found it difficult to reconcile themselves to their changed status, while some made a bid to regain power collectively through the ballot box following the creation of the Vidhan Sabha (Legislative Assembly) in 1952, Rajasthan's first democratically elected state parliament. Many of former rulers turned to business, while others converted their palaces – including the Rambagh Palace in Jaipur, the Lake Palace Hotel in Udaipur, and the Umaid Bhawan Palace in Jodhpur – into luxury hotels.

The Congress Party dominated the politics of India and held power in Rajasthan almost uninterruptedly until 1990. Congress's previous political hegemony was, however, fatally undermined during the 1990s with the emergence of the nationalistic Bharatiya Janata Party (BJP), who took control of the state legislative assembly in 1990 and have held it for considerable periods since. The BJP's populist, pro-Hindu stance has struck a chord amongst many Rajasthanis: during state elections in 2013 they captured 163 of the 200 constituencies available; while in 2014, they won every single one of

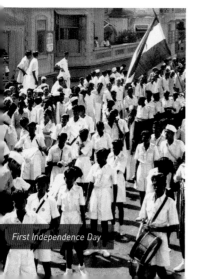

First Independence Day

Rajasthan's 25 parliamentary seats.

CONTEMPORARY RAJASTHAN

Rajasthan has come a long way since Independence. In 1947 the state had a population of 15.2 million, of whom fewer than 9 percent were literate. The popula-

Jaipur Metro

One sign of the changing times was provided by the opening of the Jaipur Metro rapid transit system in 2015, providing state-of-the-art relief to the booming city's overstretched transport infrastructure.

tion has now risen to around 70 million, with an average literacy rate of 66 percent, with 79 percent of males and 52 percent of females able to read. At the time of Independence, there was only one university in the state; there are now nine, along with around 250 colleges, 40 engineering colleges, 23 polytechnics and over 150 Industrial Training Institute (ITIs).

Major industrial development has taken place in parts of the state, particularly around Alwar, now integrated into the booming National Capital Region, and Kota, home to a cluster of hydro, thermal, gas and atomic power plants, along with one of Asia's largest fertilizer plants. The discovery of a sizeable oil field containing an estimated one billion barrels near Barmer in 1999 also provided a welcome economic boost, while tourism has also provided an increasingly important source of income. Even so, according to a report published in 2014, Rajasthan ranks amongst India's poorer states, in terms of a range of basic amenities, while essential healthcare is also frequently lacking, especially in rural areas. The constant threat of drought still hangs over large parts of the region, although the launch of the ambitious Mukhyamantri Jal Swavlamban Abhiyan (MJSA) scheme, in 2016, is already showing positive results, with the aim of making the state drought-free by 2020.

For the time being, Rajasthan remains a land of startling social contrasts. In Jaipur and Jodhpur, millionaire business-men do business deals over cocktails in luxury palace-hotels. Elsewhere, the state's illiterate villagers continue to eke out a subsistence existence amidst the desert. Such flagrant ine-qualities have been the stuff of Rajasthani life for centuries, and are unlikely to disappear anytime soon.

☉ DROUGHT IN THE DESERT

Much of Rajasthan is arid semi-desert, meaning that for cen-turies the region has remained amongst the poorest in the country. Attempts to improve the lot of Rajasthan's farmers were eventually made with the opening of the **Indira Gandhi Canal** in 1983, carrying water from the Punjab to the heart of the Thar Desert and allowing the cultivation of numerous crops in areas previously covered with sand.

Despite such measures, the ever-present threat of **drought** continues to hang over much of the state, while climate change has resulted in increasingly scarce and erratic mon-soons. Farmers have been forced off their land and wells have dried up, while viciously high temperatures in 2016 saw 19 of the state's 33 districts affected by drought. The launch, in 2016, of the **Mukhyamantri Jal Swavlamban Abhiyan** (MJSA) scheme, based on extensive new rainwater harvesting and conservation initiatives, aims to provide a lasting solution to the problem and has already scored notable successes, al-though whether it succeeds in its ambitious aim of making Rajasthan drought-free by the year 2020 is another matter.

HISTORICAL LANDMARKS

2500–1700 BC Harappan culture, the first organised society to flourish in Rajasthan, arrives.

734 Founding of the Sisodia Dynasty of Mewar, with its capital at Chittaurgarh.

1160s The Chauhan Rajputs of Ajmer emerge as the dominant local power, ruling as far as Delhi.

1191 Prithviraj Chauhan is defeated by Muhammad Ghori. Delhi falls to the Muslims.

1206 Foundation of the Delhi Sultanate are put in place.

1301 The Sultan of Delhi, Allauddin Khalji, sacks Chittaurgarh.

1459 The Rathor ruler Rao Jodha moves his capital from Mandore to Jodhpur.

1526 Babur defeats the Sultan of Delhi; the Mughal Empire is founded.

1712 Rajput states are forced to become protectorates of the increasingly powerful Maratha Empire.

1815–18 The British destroy Maratha power. The Rajput states sign 'Treaties of Friendship' with the new European rulers.

1857 The 1857 Uprising, during which most Rajput rulers remain loyal to the British.

1915 Mahatma Gandhi returns from South Africa and leads the Independence movement.

1947 India achieves Independence but is partitioned into India and Pakistan. The Rajput states join with India, forming the United State of Greater Rajasthan.

1956 Ajmer joins the United State of Greater Rajasthan, which is renamed Rajasthan.

1970 Indira Gandhi abolishes the privileges of Rajasthan's royal families.

1986 The Indira Gandhi Nahar (Canal) Project to irrigate Rajasthan is completed.

2016 Launch of the government's Mukhyamantri Jal Swavlamban Abhiyan (MJSA) scheme, aiming to make Rajasthan drought free by 2020.

2018 In May, dust storms wreak havoc in northern India killing at least 125 people, including 35 in Rajasthan.

Indian women carrying water
from stepwell near Jaipur

WHERE TO GO

Most visitors approach Rajasthan from Delhi, entering the state at Jaipur, which has excellent railway connections and is the starting point for further journeys north into Shekhawati, south to Ranthambore and Bundi, or northeast to Bharatpur (which can also be easily reached from Agra). From here, the main tourist trail continues west through Pushkar and Ajmer and onto Jodhpur and Jaisalmer before turning south to Udaipur, which is the route followed in this section.

In most parts of the state, trains provide the easiest and most memorable way of getting around, although there are a few journeys for which buses are quicker. Two weeks is just about sufficient to see Rajasthan's major highlights, while three weeks will allow you to explore at a more leisurely pace, and perhaps take in some of the state's remoter and lesser-visited attractions. Whatever you do, don't under-estimate the size of Rajasthan. India's largest state, the region covers an area roughly the size of France, and getting from A to B will consume a significant part of your time, however you approach your visit.

JAIPUR

Big, busy and brash, **Jaipur ❶** is Rajasthan's capital, largest city and economic powerhouse. The manic traffic and dense crowds deter some visitors, although the city more than compensates with a stellar array of attractions, including the opulent **City Palace**, the quirky **Jantar Mantar Observatory** and the iconic **Hawa Mahal** – not to mention the superb **Jaigarh Fort** at nearby Amber. Most of all, it is the busy streets and colour-saturated bazaars of the Pink City that linger longest in the memory – a snapshot of Indian city life at its exuberant, energetic best.

The City Palace

Jaipur is a relative newcomer by Rajasthani standards. The city was founded by Kachchwaha ruler Jai Singh II, who in 1727 moved his residence from the ancestral Kachchwaha seat of Amber Fort to a nearby location, straddling the Ajmer to Agra highway, laying out the streets of his new city in a neatly ordered grid-plan inspired by ancient Hindu architectural treatises.

At the heart of Jai Singh's carefully planned city lies the **City Palace A** (9.30am–5.30pm). The main entrance is through the grand **Tripolia** (triple-arched gate), although this is now only used by Jaipur aristocracy on festive occasions. Lesser mortals enter through **Atish Pol** around the side, passing **Chandni Chowk** (Moonlight Square), a small courtyard that is home to the palace's stables, before reaching the heart of the palace.

The complex is arranged around two main courtyards featuring a flamboyant array of buildings mingling both Hindu and Mughal styles. The larger of the two courtyards is centred on the pale yellow **Mubarak Mahal** of 1900, now housing a selection of historic clothes and textiles, including various lavish costumes made for former rulers. Close by, the **Sileh Khana** (armoury) showcases one of India's finest collections of weaponry.

Continue between a pair of imposing marble elephants through **Singh Pol** (Lion Gate), whose large bronze double doors lead into the second of the two main courtyards. The frilly white arches on the salmon-pink walls are very much in the Rajput tradition, but the **Diwan-i-Khas** (Private Audience

Hall) in the centre of the courtyard is firmly Mughal in style. Within its scalloped arches stand two huge water jars, the largest single pieces of silver in the world, made for Madho Singh II, who ruled from 1880–1920, to store water from the Ganges during his visit to Britain for the coronation of Edward VII. The **Diwan-i-Am** (Public Audience Hall) on the east side of the courtyard was built for court ceremonies, with carved screens allowing the ladies of the palace to watch proceedings unseen.

On the west side of the courtyard, **Ridhi Sidhi Pol** leads to the intimate little **Pritam Niwas Chowk**, known as the Peacock Courtyard, with four spectacular doorways on each side that have been elaborately decorated to represent the four seasons. Entrance to the courtyard is via the Peacock

City Palace, Jaipur

Jantar Mantar

Gate (autumn). The verdant Green Gate opposite (representing spring) is particularly lovely.

Beyond Pritam Niwas Chowk looms the seven-storey, pyramidal outline of the imposing **Chandra Mahal** (Moon Palace; closed to the public), home to the palace's royal apartments, and still used by the royal family to this day.

A short walk north of the palace stands the enduringly popular **Sri Govind Dev Ji Temple B**, family temple of the city's maharajas and housing an image of Govinda, the young Krishna, who serves as the guardian deity of the city's rulers

The Jantar Mantar and Hawa Mahal

Immediately south of the City Palace, huge geometric shapes dot the area like forgotten surrealist stage props. This is the **Jantar Mantar observatory C** (daily 9am–4.30pm; www.jantarmantar.org), Jai Singh II's open-air observatory of outsize astronomical instruments. Jai Singh built his first observatory in Delhi in 1724–27, the oldest observatory in India. Later, when governor of Agra, he built three more, at Ujjain, Varanasi and Mathura. The Jaipur set, built 1728–34, is the largest and best preserved, and continued to be used right up until the 1940s, keeping track of Jaipur's solar time, with the size of the instruments making readings accurate to within three seconds. The other instruments are less obviously practical. The large, circular Ram Yantras were used for reading altitudes and azimuths, while the dozen Rashivilayas are for calculating celestial latitudes and longitudes.

A short walk east of the City Palace brings you to the iconic **Hawa Mahal** Ⓓ (Palace of the Winds; daily 9am–4.30pm), built in 1799 as a giant grandstand from which royal ladies confined to *purdah* could survey the streets below. Its towering five-storey facade of pink sandstone is encrusted with lace-fine screens and carved balconies set around 953 niches and windows, tapering to the top three storeys, which are just a single room thick.

⊙ THE PINK CITY

Jaipur's most famous feature is the uniform pink colour of virtually every building within the old city, a feature that lends the entire centre an aesthetic uniformity and strange beauty, despite the somewhat grimy and battered appearance of many individual facades. Popular legend asserts that the city was painted pink (the traditional colour of welcoming and hospitality) to honour a visit by Britain's Prince of Wales in 1876. It's a colourful story, although at least one leading Indian historian has asserted that Jaipur was always pink, the colour being chosen by founder Jai Singh to emulate the marbled hues of the nearby imperial cities of Agra and Fatehpur Sikhri, and also to disguise the low quality construction materials used. Whatever its origin, the colour scheme has endured, and even today every homeowner in the city is obliged by law to maintain their facade in the requisite shade.

Hawa Mahal

Pink City Bazaars

Extending away to the south of the Hawa Mahal are the colour-soaked, craft-filled bazaars of Jai Singh's original city, or the Pink City as it's usually known thanks to the uniform rose-pink shade in which all its buildings are painted. Stretching south of the City Palace, **Johari Bazaar** **Ⓔ** (Jewellers' Bazaar) is one of the city's finest, stuffed with shops selling silver, jewellery and textiles. At the southern end of Johari Bazaar, **Bapu Bazaar** **Ⓕ** and its continuation **Nehru Bazaar,** are packed with endless shops, stacked high with everything from traditional floral prints to lacquer bangles. At the end of Nehru Bazaar, **Kishanpol Bazaar** is another major tie-dying area. Just past here is **Singh Pol** **Ⓖ** (Lion Gate), one of the grandest of the various gates leading into the Pink City. Running north from the gate, **Khajana Walon ka Rasta** is home to many of the city's marble carvers.

The Central Museum and around

Heading south through **New Gate** brings you out into the city's less crowded modern districts. Straight ahead are the **Ram Niwas Gardens** (daily 5am–8pm; free), centred on the imposing **Albert Hall** (www.alberthalljaipur.gov.in; daily 9am–5pm and 7–10pm; closed Mon Apr–Sept). This site now provides a home for Jaipur's rewarding **Central Museum** **Ⓗ**, which is stuffed with an eclectic array of exhibits including puppets, costumes, ivory, pottery and jewellery, plus a good selection of Mughal and Rajasthani miniature paintings.

Further down Jawaharlal Nehru Road is the quirky **SRC Museum of Indology** ❶ (24 Gangwal Park; daily 8am–6pm), a private collection containing an extraordinary medley of antiquities, curiosities and assorted bric-a-brac ranging from a bed made entirely of glass to a map of India drawn on a grain of rice.

Perched high on a ridgetop overlooking the northwest corner of the Pink City is another of Jaipur's former royal residences, **Nahargarh Fort J** (daily 6am–6pm). Built in 1734 to defend the new city, it also served as a state treasury, a retreat for Jai Singh's numerous consorts and as a home for tigers – the word Nahargarh means abode of tigers. However, there's not much to see inside the fort itself today, but the sunset views over the city are stunning.

AROUND JAIPUR

Hidden just east of the old city, the temple-filled gorge of **Galta** is the most interesting of the many sights around Jaipur, popularly known as the 'Monkey Temple' thanks to the thousands of boisterous macaque monkeys who live here, scavenging for food and swimming in the various tanks. A little further on, at the summit of the complex, the **Surya** Temple offers yet more stunning city views.

Water Palace

En route to Amber, look out for the magical **Jalmahal** (Water Palace), seemingly floating on the water of **Man Sagar lake**. Once used for aristocratic duck-shooting parties, the palace was neglected for many years but has now been comprehensively renovated, although it's not yet open to visitors.

Some 6km (4 miles) north of Jaipur, **Gaitor** is home to the Kachchwaha royal cremation ground (daily 9am–4pm), with the white marble *chatris* (cenotaphs) of Jaipur's rulers, including that of Jai Singh II himself, majestically silhouetted against Nahargarh hill and fort.

Amber Fort

Jaipur's story actually begin 11km (7 miles) north of the present-day city, at the magnificent **Amber Fort ❷** (daily 8am–6pm), which was for centuries the home of the powerful Kachchwaha clan before the founding of Jaipur in 1727. Their former stronghold remains one India's most magnificent: a vast pile of honey-coloured stone enclosed by miles of zigzagging walls and overlooked by the rugged **Jaigarh Fort**, perched on a hill above.

Amber Fort

As you climb up to the fort, the natural defensive advantages become increasingly clear. Entrance to the complex is through **Jai Pol** (Victory Gate), from where steps lead up to the **Kali Temple**, the Kachchwaha family shrine, built in 1604 and dedicated to Shila Mata, an aspect of Kali, the goddess of war.

Next to the temple, the huge **Singh Pol** (Lion Gate) leads to the **Diwan-i-Am** (Public Meeting Hall), set on a dazzling white terrace overlooking the valley with a double row of columns topped with elephant capitals. Diagonally opposite is magnificently colourful **Ganesh Pol gateway**, smothered in mosaic, fresco and sculpture, beyond which lies a very Mughal formal garden court. To the right is the **Sukh Nivas** (Hall of Pleasure), cooled by running water channels, while to the left is the **Jai Mandir** (Hall of Victory), Jai Singh's private apartments, blending Hindu and Mughal traditions.

The **Diwan-i-Khas** (Private Meeting Hall) is on the ground floor of the courtyard, the boldly scalloped arches giving shade to a deep veranda. Above, the gossamer-fine *jali*-work of the alabaster windows in **Jas Mandir** (Hall of Glory) are at ground level so reclining royals could enjoy the superb views. But the jewel is the **Shish Mahal** (Hall of Mirrors), its interior encrusted with tiny mirrors.

Behind the garden court lie **Man Singh's apartments**, the oldest section of the palace and concealing the *zenana* in which Man Singh's dozen wives lived, decorated with murals of Krishna and Radha.

Hovering above Amber like a watchful eagle is **Jaigarh Fort** (daily 9.30am–5pm). Built by Jai Singh II in 1726, Jaigarh formerly housed the legendary Kachchwaha treasury as well as a prodigious selection of weaponry including the massive **Jaiwan cannon**, one of the largest in Asia, capable of firing on enemies up to 20km (13 miles) distant.

SHEKHAWATI

Spread out across the arid region of semi-desert north of Jaipur, the **Shekhawati region** is one of Rajasthan's most magical surprises, dotted with a string of small, dusty towns packed with an unexpected treasure trove of spectacular havelis. The havelis themselves offer a vivid memento of the region's wealthy mercantile past, while added interest is provided by the profusion of quirky murals with which many are decorated. Mandawa and Nawalgarh are the two main centres, located close to one another at the heart of the region, while myriad other decaying havelis line the streets of Fatehpur, the provincial capital of Jhunjhunu, and numerous other

⊙ MARWARIS, MANSIONS AND MURALS

Shekhwati is famous as the home of the entrepreneurial Marwari merchants, who grew wealthy on the caravan routes crossing the Shekhawati desert and later established a business empire stretching across the whole of India. From distant Madras, Bombay (now Mumbai) and Calcutta, successful Marwari businessmen sent much of their wealth back to their ancestral homelands, building the innumerable extravagant havelis that still dot the region. Many of the havelis are also decorated with enjoyably cartoonish murals. The oldest are devoted to mainly religious themes, although later paintings often feature contemporary early 20th-century European fashions and inventions, featuring depictions of the latest British ladies' dresses alongside state-of-the-art contrivances including railways, telephones, steamships and the occasional aeroplane.

small towns and villages between.

MANDAWA AND AROUND

At the heart of the Shekhawati region, the small town of **Mandawa ❸** is the most region's most visited, and is dominated by one of the area's finest forts. Now transformed into the upmarket Castle Mandawa hotel, the building dates back to the time of the town's founding in

Beautiful old haveli in Mandawa

the mid-1750s, with three large gates leading into the cannon-guarded interior.

The streets around the fort are dotted with dozens of painted havelis in various stages of decay. On the main road through the centre of town close to the fort, the imposing **Naveti Haveli** sports entertaining early 20th-century murals featuring pictures of some of the then-latest marvels of Western technology, including the Wright brothers' aeroplane and a man using a telephone.

A ten-minute walk west of here along the main road, the **Nand Lal Murmuria** and **Goenka havelis** are particularly fine, as is the **Thakurji Mandir** opposite. Dilapidated *chatris* (cenotaphs) and a large step well line the road beyond.

Due north of Mandawa, **Mahansar** is the small but spectacular **Soni ki Dukan Haveli** (Gold Shop Haveli), its main room exquisitely decorated with paintings depicting the exploits of

Vishnu, highlighted with lavish quantities of gold leaf. The **Raghunath temple**, just down the road, boasts further fine murals.

NAWALGARH AND AROUND

Around 32km (20 miles) south of Mandawa, the fascinating town of **Nawalgarh** ❹ boasts dozens of haveli-lined streets radiating out from the old **Bala Qila fort**, right in the centre of town. Largely invisible between the surrounding houses and bazaar, the fort houses a beautiful mirrorwork encrusted Sheesh Mahal, its ceiling decorated with aerial views of Nawalgarh and Jaipur.

North of the centre lie some of Nawalgarh's most impressive havelis. The **Ath Haveli** (Eight Havelis) were built by eight brothers, although only six were ever finished. A wide range of murals adorn the buildings, including one of a steam engine and another of European ladies taking a ride in a very early automobile.

On the opposite side of town, the **Podar Haveli Museum** (www.podarhavelimuseum.org; daily summer 8am–8pm, winter 8.30am–6.30pm) occupies an immaculately restored old mansion of 1920. Unlike the faded old murals on other buildings, the pictures here have been recently repainted, showing what Shekhawati's havelis would originally have looked like in all their multi-coloured splendour.

Some 20km (12 miles) southeast of Nawalgarh, the village of **Parasrampura** has more magnificent frescoes adorning the interior of the **Gopinath Temple** and inside the dome of the *chatri* **of Rajul Singh** (donation). Close by is the delightful town of **Dundlod**, whose rugged **fort**, dating back to 1765, has been transformed into the atmospheric Dundlod Fort hotel.

Just north of Dundlod, **Mukundgarh** is built around a temple square outside the sloping fort walls. The **fort** itself has now been transformed into another atmospheric heritage hotel too, while the nearby **Kanoria, Saraf** and **Ganeriwala havelis** are also worth a look.

JHUNJHUNU

Roughly 25km (16 miles) northeast of Mandawa is the busy district capital of **Jhunjhunu** ❺, the largest town in Shekhawati and perhaps best known for its **Rani Sati Mandir**, a large temple complex, dedicated to the gruesome cult of the *sati* – widows who immolate themselves on their husband's funeral pyre.

Back in the centre of town, the old **Futala Bazaar** has a strongly Muslim flavour and boasts a further plethora of

Jhunjhunu

painted havelis. The highlight here is the **Khetri Mahal**, a beautiful open-side sandstone palace constructed in 1760 and decorated with Mughal-style cusped arches, although it's now abandoned and dilapidated. A wide ramp leads up to the roof, with views over to the sturdy **Badalgarh Fort**, built by the town's former Muslim rulers in the 16th century. Notable havelis include the two **Modi Havelis**, while immediately east of Futala Bazaar, Nehru Bazaar is home to the impressive **Bihari Mandir**, with murals dating back to the 1770s. A short walk north, the **Mertani Baori step-well** is one of Shekhawati's finest.

FATEHPUR AND AROUND

The crumbling town of **Fatehpur** ❻, 25km (15 miles) north-east of Mandawa, sees relatively few tourists but has a further

A contemporary mural, Fatehpur

slew of magnificent havelis. The frescoes on the **Devra Lal** and **Singhania havelis** are particularly fine, as are the later, more hybrid examples decorating the two **Bhartia havelis**, with mirrorwork-adorned entrances and Japanese tiles sporting pictures of Mount Fuji.

Nearby **Ramgarh**, 20km (12 miles) north of Fatehpur, is one of Shekhawati's most perfectly preserved towns, with quiet, dusty streets lined with incongruously grand but increasingly dilapidated havelis and temples, many of them decorated with the symbol – three fish joined at the mouth – of the wealthy local Poddar clan. Many of the family are buried in the extravagant sequence of **Poddar** *chatris* lining the road beyond Churu Gate. Squeezed amongst the *chatris*, the **Ganga** and **Ganesh temples** sport further murals, while the nearby **Shani Mandir** is particularly beautiful, with mirrorwork sparkling on every available surface.

NORTHEASTERN RAJASTHAN

Rajasthan's eastern extremities, almost within touching distance of Delhi and Agra, are something of a transition zone between the deserts of Rajasthan and the more agricultural and heavily populated areas over the border in the states of Uttar Pradesh and Haryana. The main draw is the idyllic Keoladeo National Park at Bharatpur, one of India's premier birdwatching destinations. There are further natural diversions at the Sariska Tiger Reserve, while the absorbing town of Alwar also attracts a smattering of visitors.

ALWAR

Guarding the northeastern-most fringes of Rajasthan is the small city of **Alwar** ❼, shielded from the desert by some

Moosi Maharani Ki Chhatri

of the highest hills in the craggy Aravalli range. Boasting a population of around 350,000, Alwar is now one of Rajasthan's major industrial centres and has been designated part of India's National Capital Region (NCR), with increasingly strong transport and business connections to Delhi, just 160km/100 miles away. The town sees few foreign visitors but has plenty of interest, with a slew of crowded bazaars, an atmospherically dilapidated city palace and the indomitable Bala Qila fort.

At the heart of the old city is the magnificent but dilapidated **City Palace**, now turned into the offices of Alwar's district government. Some of the objects owned by the erstwhile royal family are displayed in the small **museum** (daily 10am–5pm) on the palace's top floor. Below the palace sits a huge tank, lined by a chain of temples on one side and cradled in the lap of high hills, crowned by the ramparts of the Bala Qila fort. Dominating the tank is the Indo-Islamic style **Musi Maharani Chatri** cenotaph commemorating a former royal mistress, who performed *sati* here.

Further afield, on a high cliff overlooking the city, stands the rugged **Bala Qila** fort. One of oldest and wildest in the state, the fort is encircled by miles of crenellated walls zigzagging across rugged wooded hills. A steep road leads up to the dilapidated fort building itself, from where there are the spectacular views over the city, 300 metres (1,000ft) below.

SARISKA TIGER RESERVE

Some 34km (21 miles) south of Alwar on the main highway to Jaipur, the **Sariska Tiger Reserve 8** (daily 6am–4pm) protects one of the few remaining pockets of forest in the Aravalli range. The park became embroiled in arguably India's biggest-ever conservation scandal in 2005 when it was discovered that poachers had succeeded in killing every single tiger in the reserve. A number of tigers were reintroduced into the park in 2008 and 2009. However, one was later found poisoned, while several of the new tigers came from the same parents, leading to fears that any future offspring would be stunted by inbreeding and incapable of surviving in the wild. Notwithstanding these concerns, five tiger cubs have recently been sighted, bringing the reserve's number of big cats up to 18 at the time of writing, in October 2018. Whether they survive the fate of their predecessors, however, remains to be seen.

Tigers or no tigers, the Sariska reserve remains a peaceful natural sanctuary, and although you're highly unlikely to see any big cats, there is plenty of other wildlife on view. The dry, open deciduous and thorn forests support increasing populations of ungulates including sambar, nilgai, chinkara, chausingha and chital, while predators include elusive leopard, hyena, jungle cat and jackal.

BHARATPUR

An enjoyable place to recharge batteries away from the roller-coaster pace of life in Rajasthan's big cities is the small town of **Bharatpur** ❾, which offers world-class birdwatching at the peaceful **Keoladeo National Park** and an old centre featuring one of the region's most impressive forts.

Although most visitors to Bharatpur come principally to spend time at Keoladeo, the town itself is one of the most interesting in eastern Rajasthan, spreading around the mighty **Lohagarh Fort**. The fort takes its name ("Iron Fort") from its supposedly impregnable defences, which formerly included an 11-km (7-mile) -long outer wall. Inside, you can still see the fort's original trio of palaces, a beautiful set of *hamams* (baths) and two soaring towers: the **Jawahar Burj**, built in 1765 to commemorate a successful assault on Delhi, and the **Fateh Burj**, erected to commemorate the successful defence of Bharatpur from British attack in 1805.

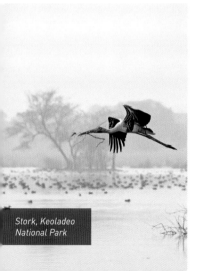

Stork, Keoladeo National Park

A number of other sights dot the streets around Bharatpur's bustling bazaar. Immediately south of the fort is the striking **Ganga Mandir** temple, dedicated to the goddess of India's most sacred river. Work on the temple began in 1845 during the rule of Maharaja Balwant Singh but wasn't finished until over 90 years later due to the astronomical construction costs. Close by, it's also worth searching out the **Jami**

Masjid (Friday Mosque) in the main bazaar, and the imposing **Laxman Mandir** temple.

KEOLADEO NATIONAL PARK

Around 4km (2 miles) east of Bharatpur town, the **Keoladeo National Park ⑩** (daily 8am–5pm) is one of India's premier birdwatching destinations, home to a huge variety of resident and migratory species, including spectacular arrays of aquatic avifauna. A metalled road runs through the park from the north gate near the main Agra–Jaipur road, with vehicles allowed only as far as the tourist and forest lodges. Beyond here, a network of raised paths along tree-lined *bunds* gives good cover for birdwatching and visitors can walk along them through much of the park.

The best time to visit is during the winter, from the end of the monsoon in October through to March, when numerous migratory species descend on the park and bird numbers are at their highest. These include thousands of water birds such as painted storks, spoonbills, cormorants, egrets, open-billed storks, purple herons, night herons and the rare sarus crane, while from October onwards migratory species arrive from the high plateaus of central Asia, Mongolia and Siberia, ranging from geese and waders to golden eagles and ospreys.

DEEG

Around 34km (22 miles) north of Bharatpur, the dusty little agricultural town of **Deeg** (or Dig) **⑪** is justly famous for its incongruously lavish **palace complex** (Sat–Thu 9am–5pm), with a string of ornate royal pavilions set amidst elegantly stylized gardens. Many of the complex's fittings were looted from Delhi and Agra in the mid-18th century by local Jat ruler Suraj Mal, which explains the palace's unexpectedly refined

Book in advance

The park's popularity means that transport is in short supply. To avoid disappointment it's a good idea to reserve a seat on a jeep or canter well in advance, either directly through your hotel (expect to pay a surcharge) or on-line at http://fmdss.forest.rajasthan.gov.in.

appearance in this rural backwater

Entering the complex you first see the imposing **Gopal Bhawan of** 1763, poised photogenically above the waters of the **Gopal Sagar** tank. Two smaller pavilions (Sawan and Bhadon – named after the two monsoon months), stand to either side, designed, with their curved roofs and pillars, to resemble a large pleasure barge, and fronted by a pair of marble thrones.

A pair of audience halls – the **Nand** and **Krishna Bhawans** – rise symmetrically on the northern and southern sides of the gardens, while at the centre is the **Keshav Bhawan** pillared summer pavilion overlooking Rup Sagar tank to the east. At the complex's southwestern corner is **Suraj Bhawan,** built of white marble and decorated with a mosaic and inlay of semi-precious stones.

SOUTHEASTERN RAJASTHAN

Stretching between Jaipur and the borders of Madya Pradesh, southeastern Rajasthan stands slightly off the main tourist trail but features several of the state's leading attractions. Pride of place goes to the world-famous **Ranthambore National Park**. Further south, peaceful **Bundi**, with its perfectly preserved haveli-lined streets, is one of Rajasthan's most enjoyable small towns, while heading east brings you to most enjoyable small towns, while heading east brings you to the huge and haunting remains of **Chittorgarh**, the most historic of all Rajput forts.

RANTHAMBORE

Around 170km (105 miles) south of Jaipur, the dusty town of **Sawai Madhopur** acts as the gateway to the world-famous **Ranthambore National Park** ⑫ (daily Oct–June), one of the best places on the planet to spot wild tigers in their natural environment. Although most tigers are predominantly nocturnal, those at Ranthambore have become increasingly diurnal over the years, often hunting by day, and the sight of one of these majestic creatures padding sedately through the

Bengal tiger, Ranthambore National Park

Tours of the national park last approximately three hours and leave either early in the morning or in mid-afternoon. Transport is aboard either a jeep ('gypsy') or a canter (open-top bus). Sightings are of course by no means guaranteed and if you're desperate to see a tiger you might consider visiting the park more than just once.

The sanctuary was originally founded in 1955, encompassing a large area which was formerly protected as a hunting area by the maharajas of Jaipur. Despite facing many difficulties, Ranthambore has successfully avoided the scandals that have plagued other Indian parks such as the nearby Sariska Tiger Reserve, which lost its entire population of big cats to poachers during the mid-2000s. Ranthambore's tiger population has grown steadily over the past decade, from around

Jackal at Ranthambore National Park

poachers during the mid-2000s. Ranthambore's tiger population has grown steadily over the past decade, from around 25 in 2005 to around 70 at current estimates, a result of stringent anti-poaching measures and incentives to keep local villagers out of the park.

Ranthambore's major predator is of course the tiger, while the park is also home to leopards, jackals and hyena, along

Ranthambore Fort

with elusive caracal and jungle cats. Many ungulates roam the park, providing the tigers with their prey. Other resident animals include the marsh crocodile, wild boar, ratel, monitor lizard and the cute, insect-eating sloth bear (although they can become unexpectedly ferocious – even the tigers usually avoid them). Look out, too, for the famous banyan near Jogi Mahal at the base of the fort, reputedly the second-largest in the world.

Often overlooked by visitors, the nearby **Ranthambore Fort** (daily 6am–6pm; free) is another major attraction, with its mighty walls rising some 250 metres (800ft) from the floor of the forested valley. Dating back to the 5th century, this is one of the most ancient – and impregnable – forts in Rajasthan, and was never taken in battle, although it witnessed many sieges over its 800-year history. The fort sits on a rugged hill running east to west. Massive ramparts, crenellations, mighty gates and bastions have been built

Bundi City Palace

all around the hill, rising straight from near-vertical cliffs and rocks, while dozens of old buildings survive, scattered across the huge flat summit, including the **Badal Mahal** (Palace of the Clouds), the 84-columned cenotaph of Hamir Deva, and ancient **temples** dedicated to Shiva and Ganesh –the latter attracts thousands of local visitors during the annual Ganesh Chaturthi festival.

BUNDI

Tucked away in the southeastern fringes of Rajasthan southwest of Ranthambore, idyllic **Bundi** ⑬ rivals Pushkar as Rajasthan's most popular small-town retreat, with a stunning city palace and beautiful streets still lined with their original havelis.

Dominating the old town from its hilltop is the early 16th-century **City Palace** (daily 8am–6pm), one of southern Rajasthan's purest examples of Rajput architecture. The palace is particularly famous for its superb murals, created by the school of miniature painters that flourished here between the 17th and 19th centuries. The best Bundi miniatures and murals (many showing scenes from the life of Krishna) have a unique style, with images of an almost fairytale-like vividness, the ruler's *Diwan-i-Am* (public audience chamber) and on to the living apartments of the ruler, the **Chattra Mahal**, centred on a miniature courtyard with sweeping views over the town's blue-washed buildings, which looks rather like a miniature version of Jodhpur.

Further steps ascend ever higher to reach the **Phool Mahal**, decorated in superb murals painted during the 1860s depicting a huge procession of elephants, horses, soldiers in European uniform and a unit of camel cavalry. From here, a final staircase leads up to the highest room in the palace, the fittingly named **Badal Mahal**, (Cloud Palace). The climb is rewarded by the sight of some of the finest murals in Rajasthan. A vivid circle of Krishnas and Radhas dance around the dome overhead, flanked by pictures of Ganesh driving Krishna to his wedding, and the return from Lanka of Rama at the end of the *Ramayana*, flying through the sky in his chariot, borne aloft by a quartet of winged angels.

Taragarh fort

Exit the main palace, go downhill for 20 metres (65ft) and then turn up the ramp on your left to reach the 18th-century **Chittra Sala**. This open quadrangle, surrounded by cloistered galleries, is home to a further superb selection of paintings, depicting scenes from the life of Krishna along with gods, heavenly damsels, and scenes from courtly life, all painted in predominantly blue-green, underwater tones.

Crowning the top of a 150-metre (500-ft) hill high above the town stands the **Taragarh** (Star Fort; free), reached by a steep 20-minute uphill climb from the Chittra Sala. The fort is now largely ruined, with overgrown masonry and a large monkey population, although visitors are free to explore the remains of the fort's impressive battlements and bastions.

Also worth hunting out is the superb **Rani-ki-Baodi** stepwell of 1770, on the south side of the old town. Wide steps lead down to the water under a graceful *torana* (archway) surmounted by a frieze of elephants, while carvings showing the 10 incarnations of Vishnu line the walls.

North of Bundi lies a second lake, **Jait Sagar**, and the **Sukh Niwas** (Palace of Bliss), built in 1773 by Rao Raja Bishen Singh. Former guests include Rudyard Kipling, who, it is said, wrote parts of *Kim* during a stay here.

KOTA

Rajasthan's third-largest city, down-to-earth **Kota** ⑭ offers a gritty reminder of modern India's industrial realities amidst the fairy-tale cities of Rajasthan, although the lavish City Palace provides a reminder of older and more traditional times. With over one million inhabitants, Kota is now one of Rajsthan's leading industrial centres thanks to its location situated next to the Chambal River, which provides an abundant supply of water along with electricity generated by the hydro, atomic and thermal power stations lined up along its banks.

Kota's main tourist attraction is the rambling **City Palace** (daily 10am–4.30pm; www.kotahfort.com). Begun in 1625, the palace was gradually extended over the years by successive rulers, evolving into a colourful confusion of courtyard,

Kota thermal power plant

pavilions, audience halls and private chambers arranged around the imposing **Jaleb Chowk** (Big Square) and the glittering **Raj Mahal**. Sections of the palace interior are open to visitors as the **Maharao Madho Singh Museum** (Sat–Thu 10am–4.30pm), showcasing the cultural heritage of the local rulers along with a fine display of miniature paintings.

Stretching northeast of the palace is the **old town** , formerly defended on three sides by a moat and massive fortified crenellated walls, and with the Chambal River forming a natural barrier to the west.

CHITTORGARH

Nowhere in Rajasthan is as redolent of history as the monumental fortress-citadel of **Chittorgarh** ⓕ (or "Chittor", as it's sometimes abbreviated), around 130km (80 miles) southwest of Bundi, or 115km (72 miles) east of Udaipur. Stretching for around 11km

(7 miles) along a lofty ridgetop, the fort was the scene of the some of the bloodiest events in the region's gory past. Former capital of the Mewar kingdom and once home to almost 100,000 people, the fort is now eerily quiet and abandoned, although many of its magnificent buildings survive in excellent condition, mute witnesses to the various horrors enacted here.

The road up to the **fort** (sunrise–sunset) zigzags steeply for just over 1km (0.6 mile), passing through seven huge *pols* (gates), each with watchtowers and great iron-spiked doors. At the top, inside the fort itself, the **Palace of Rana Kumbha** is the first large building you reach, named after Rana Kumbha, one of early Mewar's greatest rulers. The nearby **Fateh Prakash**

⊙ THE CONQUESTS OF CHITTORGARH

Despite its towering hilltop location and seemingly impregnable fortifications, Chittorgarh was overrun and sacked no less than three times in the eight centuries during which it served as Mewar capital. The first catastrophe occurred in 1303, when the fearsome Delhi Sultan Allauddin Khalji (attracted, legend says, by the beauty of the ruler's wife, a certain Padmini) attacked the city, leading to the death of all the city's menfolk in battle, while the women of the city performed *jauhar* (mass *sati*), casting themselves into an enormous funeral pyre. Further calamity ensued in 1535, when sultan Bhadur Shan of Gujarat sacked the fort, and again in 1567, when the great Mughal emperor Akbar attacked Chittorgarh, leading to a devastating siege lasting almost a year. Facing defeat, the city's warriors once again rode out to die in battle, while their women performed *jauhar*, after which the city was ransacked, never to recover, and a new capital established at Udaipur.

Akbar Attacking the Fortress at Chittorgarh

Palace, built in the early 19th century, houses a small museum displaying archaeological finds from the site.

East of here is the 14th-century **Kirti Stambh** (Tower of Fame), rising imperiously above the eastern side of the fort and dedicated to Sri Adinath Rishabdeo, the first Jain *tirthankara* (enlightened one). Further south, the intricately carved **Kumbha Shyam Temple** of 1448 is dedicated to the Varaha (boar) incarnation of Lord Vishnu. A smaller temple in the same compound commemorates Mira Bai, the famous princess-poet and devotee of Krishna.

South of the here is Chittorgarh's most impressive landmark, the soaring **Vijay Stambh** (Victory Tower), a 36-metre (120ft) -high limestone tower visible from miles away. Commissioned by Rana Kumbha, the tower commemorates his victory in 1440 against the combined forces of Malwa and Gujarat. Next to the Vijay Stambh lies the sombre courtyard where the queens of Chittorgarh performed *sati*, as demonstrated by the sobering sight of countless diminutive memorial stones.

Continuing south brings you to the **Samidhisvhara Temple**, dedicated to Shiva, the **Kalika Mata temple** and, finally, to an 18th-century reconstruction of **Padmini's Palace**. A small pool lies next to the palace in which, according to legend, the rapacious Delhi Sultan Allauddin Khalji was permitted to gaze upon a reflected image of the legendary queen.

AJMER AND PUSHKAR

Almost in the dead centre of Rajasthan, the neighbouring towns

Pilgrims bathing in sacred Pushkar Lake

of Pushkar and Ajmer are two of the state's most important pilgrimage destinations, but in many other respects, could hardly be more different. The idyllic Hindu pilgrimage town of Pushkar is one of the prettiest in Rajasthan, with dozens of temples and snowy-white ghats ringing a picture-perfect lake. The town has long been one of Rajasthan's leading tourist magnets thanks to its laid-back ambience and beautiful lakeside setting, and still retains a slightly alternative, quirky atmosphere – a legacy of the flocks of wandering Western hippies and beatniks who first discovered the place during the 1970s. The much larger nearby town of Ajmer, by contrast, has a decidedly Muslim flavour thanks to the revered Dargah Sharif, and has yet to be seduced by the tourist dollar – which for many visitors is a major part of its appeal.

AJMER

The largest town between Jaipur and Jodhpur, **Ajmer** ⑯ is one of central Rajasthan's major economic hubs and also its most important place of Muslim pilgrimage. Established in the 7th century by the Chauhan Rajputs, the town remained a leading centre of Rajput power until 1191, when it was captured by Muhammad of Ghori and remaining under the control of the Delhi Sultans until 1326. After two centuries of instability it was absorbed into the Mughal Empire in 1556 by Akbar, who made Ajmer the base for his operations in the region. As such, the town's history is markedly different from that of other major urban centres in the state, with a pronounced Muslim rather than Hindu flavour, and even today it feels like the least Rajasthani town in Rajasthan.

The Dargah Sharif

At the heart of the old city, the **Dargah Sharif** (www.darga-hajmer.com; daily 5am–midnight) attracts pilgrims from across the Islamic world who come to visit the tomb of the revered Persian Sufi saint Muin-ud-din Chishti, whose message of love and devotion to the poor helped spread the word of Islam throughout the region. The Dargah sees a steady flow of pilgrims throughout the year, rising to a flood during the Urs Mela festival, celebrated during Rajab (May/June), when hundreds of thousands of pilgrims converge upon the shrine.

A food stall on Dargah Bazaar in Ajmer

Even on quiet days the Dargah has a character quite unlike the rest of Rajasthan, with *qawwals* (religious singers) chanting the saint's praises, fakirs pleading for alms, and *khadim* ('servants' of the saint) keeping a lookout for pilgrims.

The approach to the shrine is through the congested **Dargah Bazaar**, with tiny shops piled high with ritual offerings. Entrance to the shrine complex itself is through a pair of gates: the **Nizam Gate** and the **Shajanhani Gate**, the latter commissioned by Shah Jahan himself. Next to this is the **mosque** built by Akbar in thanks for the birth of his first son; past here is the 15th-century **Buland Darwaza** gateway, next to which stand two huge *deg* (cauldrons) into which pilgrims throw donations.

The simple brick **tomb** in which the saint was buried has since been embellished by the lavish gifts of wealthy devotees, with the grave now enclosed by a silver railing and partially surrounded by a marble lattice screen. Further mosques, pavilions and gateways surround the mausoleum. To its north lies the **mehfil khana**, the scene of all-night performances of *qawwali* (devotional songs). West of the mausoleum lies Shah Jahan's elegant **mosque** in white marble, while to the east is the ornate **Begami Dalan**, built by Princess Jahanara, the emperor's daughter.

Around the Dargah

West of the Dargah lies the immense **Adhai din ka Jhonpra**. Originally a Sanskrit college, it was converted into a mosque by Muhammad al Ghori in 1198 and remains one of India's finest medieval monuments, covered in ornate calligraphic inscriptions. The pillars retain Hindu elements but the screen and arches were added in 1266.

A five-minute walk northeast of the Dargah is Akbar's red sandstone palace, the **Daulat Khana,** built in 1570. The central audience hall is now the **Government Museum** (Sat–Thu 10am–5.30pm), housing an extensive collection of weaponry and sculptures from the 4th to the 12th centuries.

Just north of here is the ornate 19th-century **Nasiyan** (Red) **Jain Temple** (daily 8.30am–5.30pm). The shrine itself is closed to non-Jain visitors, but visitors are welcome in the

Pushkar Passport

Foreigners visiting the *ghats* around Pushkar Lake are traditionally asked to make a donation to one of the priests who patrol the waterside (fake priests are also common). In return, visitors receive a consecrated wrist-thread, popularly known as the 'Pushkar Passport', allowing them to explore the ghats during the rest of their stay.

remarkable hall next door, sporting a huge representation of the Jain universe, viewable from a series of galleries. A little further north lies the tranquil **Ana Sagar Lake**, ringed with a white marble embankment and pavilions commissioned by Shah Jahan.

PUSHKAR

Just 11km (7 miles) northwest of Ajmer, the small town of **Pushkar ⑰** is one of Rajasthan's most important pilgrimage destinations, attracting an endless stream of devout Hindus who come to bathe in the sacred waters of the town's small lake. Religion remains at the heart of Pushkar, despite the hordes of visiting Westerners, with a picturesque maze of ashrams (hermitages), dharamshalas (pilgrim rest houses) and around 400 temples, and one is never far from the sound of worship or the sight of ascetics and devotees. The many

◎ THE PUSHKAR CAMEL FAIR

For seven days in the month of Kartik (usually November) life in Pushkar is transformed by the vibrant Pushkar Camel Fair, held on the dunes west of the town. The fair marks the arrival of the Kartika Purnima (Kartik full moon), during which bathing in the lake is believed to be particularly auspicious. Religious celebrations, however, are now thoroughly overshadowed by the huge camel fair, one of the largest in the state, with thousands of brightly turbaned men and brilliantly dressed women arriving with their livestock to trade and celebrate, transforming the dunes into a sea of vibrant colour and strutting camels – rural Rajasthan at its most festive and flamboyant.

temples include shrines to Shiva, Badri Narayan, Varaha, Savitri and Gayatri, although pride of place goes to the great Brahma Temple in the centre of town, one of the few in India dedicated to the supreme creator of the Hindu trinity.

The lake itself is bounded by 52 *ghats*, built over the centuries by kings and nobles. Of these, the **Varaha**, **Brahma** and **Gau ghats** are the most revered. Varaha Ghat is considered especially sacred, thanks to the belief that Vishnu himself appeared here in the form of a boar.

The Jodhpur alleyways

JODHPUR

Rajasthan's second-largest city and former capital of the state of Marwar, **Jodhpur** 18 is a city of contrasts. Parts of the modern city are as hectic and traffic-plagued as anywhere in the state, and yet wandering the narrow alleyways between the blue-painted houses of the old town, the scenery and pace of life can feel almost medieval. Likewise with the city's two headline attractions: the adamantine **Meherangarh Fort**, as massive and impregnable as any in India; and the opulent **Umaid Bhawan Palace**, a supersized study in early 20th-century extravagance and excess. All of which adds up to one of

The Blue City

Jodhpur is popularly known as the 'Blue City' on account of the blue plaster in which many of the old city's houses are covered. Blue originally signified the house of a high-caste Brahmin, although the colour proved popular (and is believed to repel insects) and was widely copied across the city.

Rajasthan's most enjoyably eclectic destinations.

Meherangarh Fort

Dominating all views of the city is the vast, and very aptly named, **Meherangarh** (Majestic) **Fort** (daily 9am–5pm), Originally built by Jodhpur's founder, Rao Jodha, in 1459, Meherangarh is without doubt Rajasthan's most formidable citadel, perched on top of a lofty rock outcrop 100 metres (328ft) above the flat surrounding plains and ringed by walls reaching heights of almost 40 metres (131ft) in places.

Entrance to the fort is through the ceremonial **Jai Pol**, a late addition from 1808, from where the road twists steeply upwards through a series seven protective gates to reach **Loha** (Iron) **Pol.** Like the other gates, Loha Pol is built just after a bend so the enemy could not rush it and reinforced with iron spikes against elephant charges. The sombre handprints of 31 royal *satis* can still be seen daubed on its wall. Beyond here, a final gate, **Suraj** (Sun) **Pol**, marks the entrance to the fort's sumptuous domestic quarters.

Inside, the palace is arranged around the maharaja's public and private rooms and the *zenana* (women's quarters). Up the narrow stairs from Suraj Pol is the 16th-century **Shangar Chowk** (Coronation Courtyard). Enclosed by *jali* (lattice) work of gossamer fineness, the courtyard provides a beautiful setting for the marble **Sringar Chowki** (Coronation Seat), with peacock armrests and gilded elephants. Rooms around the

Inside, the palace is arranged around the maharaja's public and private rooms and the *zenana* (women's quarters). Up the narrow stairs from Suraj Pol is the 16th-century **Shangar Chowk** (Coronation Courtyard). Enclosed by *jali* (lattice) work of gossamer fineness, the courtyard provides a beautiful setting for the marble **Sringar Chowki** (Coronation Seat), with peacock armrests and gilded elephants. Rooms around the Shangar Chowk now serve as the fort's **museum**, filled with a spectacular collection of royal palanquins and elephant *howdahs* (seats), while beyond is the airy **Phool Mahal** (Flower Palace), with pictures of former rulers looking down from the elaborately painted and gilded ceiling.

Past here, **Takhat Vilas** contains the apartments of Maharaja Takhat Singh, who ruled from 1843–73. Colourful balls hang

Moti Mahal (Pearl Palace) is the largest period room of the Mehrangarh Museum

Sadar bazaar

room, including the ingenious mechanical cradle of the last maharaja.

The intimate **Moti Mahal** (Pearl Palace) was where councils of state were formerly held. Nine cushions lie ranged around the red-carpeted floor, each reserved for one of the state leaders, with a central cushioned dais for the maharaja himself. Alcoves in the wall opposite conceal balconies from which the women of the palace could eavesdrop on proceedings.

Beyond here visitors enter the *zenana* – a self-contained section with apartments for the ladies of the palace and roof terraces around the communal **Rang Mahal** – with exhibits including fine musical instruments and extravagant royal costumes.

On the road down from the fort, a splash of blinding white marble announces the **Jaswant Thanda** (daily 9am–5pm), the *chatri* (cenotaph) of Maharaja Jaswant Singh II, built in 1899. As with the Taj Mahal, the marble is from Makrana.

Alongside stand the *chatris* of the subsequent four Rathor rulers, including that of Umaid, creator of the famous Umaid Bhawan Palace.

The old city

Extending below the fort**, old Jodhpur** retains much of its medieval character, spreading out in a disorienting maze of twisting streets and lanes from the central **Sardar Bazaar** , with its distinctive **Clock Tower** of 1912. Palaces, havelis and temples dot the area, many with richly carved façades, while the area also provides a haven for Jodhpur's traditional artisans, such as the **Mochi** (Cobbler) **Bazaar**, busy with the regular tap-tapping of shoemakers at work and filled with shops selling colourfully embroidered slippers (*jutis*).

UMAID BHAWAN PALACE

In 1929, in the midst of a long-term famine, Maharaja Umaid Singh had the bright idea of employing 3,000 citizens a day for 16 years to build himself a playtime palace par excellence, the **Umaid Bhawan Palace** , finally completed in 1944 – one of the largest private homes in the world, and without doubt one of the most spectacular buildings of the 1930s. The resultant 347-room royal dwelling is so huge that the former royals now spread themselves

Jodhpurs

The name 'Jodhpur' is synonymous with the distinctive style of horse-riding trouser, baggy at the top, narrow at the bottom. Originally invented by Pratap Singh, brother of Jodhpur maharaja Jaswant Singh, they proved a massive hit in Britain when introduced by Pratap during a visit to attend Queen Victoria's Golden Jubilee.

airily over a third of it, run the official rooms as a museum, and are still able to leave a further 57 suites plus assorted public areas to serve as arguably the country's finest hotel. Even if you're not staying here you can visit the palace's **museum** (daily 9am–5.30pm), stuffed with luxury items acquired by the royal family alongside vivid paintings of scenes from the *Mahabharata* by the Polish artist Stephen Norblin, who designed much of the palace's interior.

MANDORE

Some 10km (6 miles) north of Jodhpur lies **Mandore, the** former capital of Marwar, until Jodhpur was founded in 1459. Mandore's crowning glory are its **six dewals**, the domed royal *chatris* (cenotaphs) of the Rathor rulers, standing amidst lush landscaped gardens. Each is built on the spot where the ruler was cremated, joined on his pyre by various wives and concubines. Starting with Rao Maldeo's fairly modest *chatri*, the monuments increase steadily in height and grandeur, neatly mirroring the rise in Marwar's fortunes.

Across the garden is the **Hall of Heroes**, with 16 life-sized figures carved out of the rock during the 18th century. The heroes are either Hindu deities or local Rajputs, mounted on horseback. The larger hall next door is the optimistically named **Shrine of 30 Crore** (3,000 million) **Gods**, crammed with huge painted statues of assorted Hindu deities. The ruins of old Mandore city and its fort litter the rocky plateau above, beyond which are some 60 further *chatris*, commemorating the wives of the royal rulers buried lower down the hill.

The Bishnoi villages

Numerous tour operators in Jodhpur offer interesting 'village safaris' into the surrounding countryside, with visits en route to the homes of some the remarkable **Bishnoi** (*bisnoi*) people. All Bishnois follow the 21 tenets laid down by the 15th-century Guru Jambeshwar, Rajasthan's original eco-warrior. This unique set of religious rules aims to promote a life lived in harmony in nature, including a fervent belief in the sanctity of all animal and plant life, particularly the sacred *khejri* tree. In 1730, 363 Bishnois at the village of

Young Indian Bishnoi woman with headscarf

Khejarli gave their lives while defending a grove of *khejri* from loggers sent by the maharaja of Johdpur. Moved by their bravery, the ruler decreed a ban on the felling of all trees and the killing of all animals in Bishnoi territory, a ban which persists to this day. Bishnoi villages are, as a result, a haven for wildlife, particularly the herds of deer that inhabit the area. Bishnois believe that they will be reincarnated as deer and are now responsible for protecting around 90 percent of the remaining blackbuck gazelles in India, along with many other species.

The villages themselves are immaculate, scrubbed daily by brightly clad women, who are weighed down with jewellery and festooned with bangles the length of their arms. By contrast, the men dress entirely in white, with loosely swathed large turbans. Visitors may also witness (or even be invited to take part in) a village **opium ceremony**, during which a kind of tea is made using opium dissolved in water.

BIKANER

The remote desert city of **Bikaner** ⓳ was formerly a major trading centre on the old caravan routes linking Central Asia and North India with the Gujarat seaports, founded in 1486 by a Rathor prince named Bika. Modern Bikaner is now a big and bustling city with a population of around 700,000. Tourism here is relatively low-key, although the old city is full of interest and it's a good place to arrange a camel trek into the Thar from, as the surrounding sands are notably quieter and less developed than the desert around Jaisalmer.

Junagarh Fort

The centrepiece of the city, **Junagarh Fort** (daily 10am–5pm), is one of the finest in Rajasthan. Interestingly, it is one of the few in India that was never conquered, despite lacking the commanding hilltop setting of the forts at Jodhpur, Jaisalmer, Amber, Chittorgarh and elsewhere.

Entrance to the fort is through the huge spiked gates of Daulat Pol, opposite which is a wall covered with the handprints of women who committed *sati* here. Continue up into the intimate Vikram Vilas courtyard, beyond which is the fort's main courtyard, surrounded by some of the palace's oldest and most beautiful rooms, including the exquisitely decorated 17th-century **Karan Mahal**.

Punkah

Dangling from the ceiling of the Karan Mahal you'll see a traditional *punkah*, a kind of fan operated by a rope pulled by a special servant, the *punkah-wallah*, which was the best that even the rulers of Rajasthan enjoyed in the way of air-conditioning before the advent of electricity.

The enclosed area beyond Karan Mahal conceals the lovely **Rai Niwas**, the oldest part of the palace, cooled by a white marble pool. The nearby dazzling **Anup Mahal** served as the palace's *Diwan-i-Khas* (Hall of Public Audience), complete with ruler's throne and richly woven carpet. The contrastingly understated **Badal Mahal** (Cloud Palace) nearby sports chaste blue motifs inspired by rain clouds – something rarely seen in arid Bikaner. Upstairs the **Gaj Mandir Shish Mahal** (Hall of Mirrors), with its ivory-inlaid bed and inviting swing-seat, seems ready and waiting for its royal master.

Anup Mahal

From here, visits proceed into more modern parts of the fort centred on the 20th-century Ganga Niwas. The huge **Ganga Niwas Durbar Hall** formerly provided a splendid setting for royal ceremonies and now houses, unexpectedly, a complete World War I-era De Havilland biplane. The maharaja's office next door is a perfectly preserved early 20th-century period piece.

Just outside the main fort, the **Prachina Museum** (daily 9am–6pm) houses a colourful collection of early 20th-century luxury items amassed by the ruling family.

The old city

Bikaner's walled **old city** comprises a fascinating labyrinth of narrow roads and alleyways still ringed by imposing bastions

Lallgarh Palace

and a number of impressive gates including the main entrance, **Kote Gate**, surrounded by a sea of bustling bazaars.

Things are much quieter inside the city walls. Several lovely havelis dot the streets here – tricky to find, but worth the effort. Bikaner's havelis are notably different from those elsewhere in Rajasthan: many date from the early years of the 20th century and mix traditional Rajasthani motifs with popular European designs, including Art Deco and Art Nouveau, to create an eclectic and sometimes slightly outlandish hybrid architectural style. The easiest to find are the three grand **Rampuria Havelis** (continue past Kote Gate and continue down the small road directly past the City Kotwali administrative offices), their facades decorated with images ranging from Krishna to King George V. Further into the old city, other notable havelis include the extravagant **Kothari Building**, with flamboyant Art Nouveau exterior, and the **Punan Chand Haveli**, with funky floral facade.

AROUND BIKANER

Set in the open countryside around 2.5km (1.5 miles) north of the centre, the **Lallgarh Palace** was built in 1900 for Maharaja Ganga Singh mixing Orientalist fantasy and European luxury. The palace now houses a pair of upmarket hotels (the Laxmi

Niwas and the Lallgarh Palace), along with the **Shri Sadul Museum** (Mon–Sat 10am–5pm), housing a vast collection of royal bric-a-brac including hundreds of historic photographs.

Further afield, around 11km (7 miles) east of the centre at **Devi Kund Sagar**, stand the marble and sandstone *chatris* (cenotaphs) of Bikaner's rulers, packed tightly together in a small enclosure set next to a large artificial tank. The mausoleum dates back to the rule of Rai Singh, creator of Junagarh, who is buried here along with all 19 of the city's subsequent rulers.

Bikaner's desert heritage is to the fore at the **National Research Centre of Camels** (usually known simply as 'the camel farm'; daily 2–6pm), 10km (6 miles) south of town. This unique camel breeding farm is famed for its quality dromedaries: the best are snapped up by the military; others are sold for

---

⊙ THE REINCARNATION OF SACRED RODENTS

The rats of Deshnok are considered sacred thanks to a legend connected to Karni Mata herself. According to one legend, the saint's own stepson, Laxman, drowned in a pool, after which Karni Mata descended into the underworld to ask Yama, god of the dead, to restore the boy. Yama eventually relented, agreeing to bring Laxman back to life as a rat, along with all Karni Mata's future male descendants. Another legend says that an army of fleeing soldiers asked for the saint's aid. Knowing that they faced death for deserting the battlefield, she promptly transformed them into rats and offered them the sanctuary of her temple. The rodents you see at Deshnok are therefore considered the reincarnated souls of her descendants or devotees, and worshipped as such.

local domestic use. There are usually around 200 camels at the centre, where you can also spot cute baby camels and take a camel ride. Feeding time (daily from 3.30pm) is the best part of the day to visit.

Karni Mata Temple

Some 30km (19 miles) south of Bikaner at the village of Deshnok stands the unique **Karni Mata Temple** (daily 4.30am–10pm; free but camera and video charge), dedicated to the 15th-century mystic Karni Mata. The temple is famous for the sacred rats (*kabas* – there are an estimated 20,000 in total), which inhabit every corner of the temple, scurrying across the floor and sitting in corners eating and drinking food and milk donated by devotees. Food nibbled by the rats is considered

Jain temples complex in Jaisalmer

consecrated, and leftovers are often taken away by pilgrims for their own consumption.

JAISALMER

Even in a land of magical palaces and fairy-tale forts, **Jaisalmer ⑳** is extraordinary. Rising like a mirage out of the endless scrub of the Thar Desert, the city seems almost untouched by the modern world: a flawless ensemble of honey-coloured fort, temples and havelis which appears to have sprung magically out of the sands as if in some Arabian Nights fable. Even close at hand the mirage persists, from the fort's soaring bastions, sumptuous Maharawal's Palace and exquisite Jain temples through to the eye-bogglingly decorated havelis in the town below.

Jaisalmer Fort

The ancestral home of the ruling Bhati clan, Jaisalmer was founded in 1156 by Rawal Jaisal. Abandoning his palace at nearby Lodurva, Jaisal established a new and much more easily defensible rock-top citadel, **Jaisalmer Fort Ⓐ**, perched atop the largest hill for miles around and contained within double ramparts rising almost 100 metres (325ft) above the surrounding countryside.

Entering the fort through **Ganesh Pol** from Manik Chowk (main market) a steep flag-stoned incline leads up past **Suraj Pol**, the Sun Gate to **Bhointa Pol**, the Turn Gate, its name later corrupted to **Bhoota Pol**, the Haunted Gate, on account of the many bloody fights seen here. A final gate, **Hawa Pol**, the Wind Gate, leads to the main square within the fort, known as Dussehra Chowk, or simply **Main Chowk**.

Dominating the square is the stately **Palace of the Maharawal** Ⓑ, former residence of the city's rulers, whose soaring, richly carved facade is amongst the finest in Rajasthan. Much of the interior is now open as the **Fort Palace Museum** (daily 8am–5.30pm) with a sequence of richly decorated rooms, although built on a far smaller scale than other royal palaces around the state. A flight of marble steps facing the palace on the left leads up to an imposing white marble throne from which the ruler once issued his decrees.

The Jain Temples

Heading further into the fort brings you to an extensive group of seven 12th- to 15th-century **Jain temples** Ⓒ (daily 8am–noon). The finest of the seven shrines is the **Rishabdevji Temple**, entered through an intricately carved *torana* (scrolled archway). A porch supported by pillars carved with creepers and flowers leads to the main *mandapa* (hall), with columns sporting graceful heavenly nymphs, celestial dancers and musicians facing the central image of Rishabdevji. Next door is the subsidiary **Sambhavnath Temple**, smaller and simpler in design.

Linked to the Sambhavji Temple by a cloistered passage, **Ashtapadi Temple** has beautiful images of Hindu deities on the outer pillars and walls of its *mandapa* (porch-like structure), while the donors who funded construction of the temple guard its entrance, seated on elephants.

The havelis

The city outside the fort is home to Rajasthan's finest array of traditional carved havelis. Largest and most elaborate of all is the **Patwon Ki Haveli** Ⓓ (House of the Brocade

Merchants), standing in a cul-de-sac with an imposing gate spanning the entrance to the lane. Begun in 1800, the haveli, which consists of five separate, interlinked suites, took 50 years to complete. Two of the five sections of the haveli are open to the public as the **Kothari Patwa Haveli Museum** (daily 9am–5pm), complete with traditional period furnishings.

Close by, the **Nathmalji Ki Haveli E** (daily 9am–7pm; free) is the newest of the great Jaisalmer havelis, built in the late 19th century for the Nathmalji, the state prime minister. Further east down the central Bhatia Bazaar is **Salim Singh's Haveli F** (daily 8am–6pm), instantly recognizable thanks to its unusual cantilevered upper storey, supported by carved peacock brackets.

Barra Bagh cenotaph

AROUND JAISALMER

Scattered across a rocky eminence 6km (4 miles) west of Jaisalmer, the *chatris* (cenotaphs) of the former Bhati rulers of Jaisalmer stand at **Barra Bagh** (daily sunrise–sunset). A pillared and canopied *chatri*, many built of white marble, marks the site of each ruler's cremation, while the garden also offers spectacular desert sunsets.

Further afield, some 16km (10 miles) northwest of Jaisalmer, is **Lodurva**, former capital of the Bhati rulers. The ancient township now lies in ruins, although the site remains an important place of Jain pilgrimage thanks to its various temples. The main **Parshvananth Temple** (dedicated to the 23rd *thirthankara*) is one of the finest in the state, with a profusion of detailed sandstone carvings covering every surface and a flamboyant

Sam sand dunes

entrance porch balanced on an unusual triangular arch.

THE THAR DESERT

The beautiful desert scenery around Jaisalmer is a major local attraction, although increasingly large visitor numbers mean that many parts of the wilderness are no longer as pristine as they once were, and the most popular places can get overrun with crowds.

> ### Camel safaris
>
> Top of many Jaisalmer visitors' wish lists is the chance to go on a local camel safaris, enjoying the memorable experience of rolling on camel-back through the sands and spending a night under a huge canopy of stars. For more information, see the section on Camel Trekking in the What to Do section, p.96.

The famous sand dunes at **Sam**, 40km (25 miles) west of town, continue to pull in the crowds but have now largely disappeared beneath a succession of huge tented camps and the feet of thousands of visitors. Another popular, and somewhat quieter, desert destination is the small and still relatively unspoilt village of **Khuri**, 40km (25 miles) south of town, with traditional thatched mudbrick houses and colourfully dressed inhabitants.

UDAIPUR AND SOUTHERN RAJASTHAN

The beautiful lakeside city of **Udaipur** ㉑, erstwhile capital of the state of Mewar, is perhaps the most captivating destination in Rajasthan, a fairy-tale ensemble of snowy-white buildings clustered around idyllic Lake Pichola. Udaipur is also the best starting point for excursions to the exquisite Jain temples of **Ranakpur** and the huge fort of **Kumbulgarh**, while further south there are more Jain temples and appealingly rugged upland scenery at the hill resort of **Mount Abu**.

LAKE PICHOLA

The photogenic centrepiece of old Udaipur, picture-perfect **Lake Pichola** Ⓐ provides the city with plentiful water, cooling breezes and of course, many of its most memorable views. The jewel of the lake is without doubt the magical Jag Niwas Palace, a former royal residence now transformed into the world-famous **Lake Palace Hotel**, clad in pure white stucco and appearing to float magically upon the waters of the lake. Unfortunately it's only open to hotel guests, meaning that unless you are able to afford a room here, you'll have to make do with admiring it from a distance.

The second of Lake Pichola's two island-palaces is the **Jag Mandir,** constructed, according to tradition, as a retreat for Prince Khurram, the future Mughal Emperor Shah Jahan. Huge seamless stone slabs of almost translucent thinness were used in the building of the main Gol Mahal building, with cupolas, a lofty dome and spacious courtyards, all surrounded by exquisite gardens.

The City Palace

Soaring high above the northeast corner of Lake Pichola is Udaipur's incomparable **City Palace** Ⓑ (daily 9.30am–5.30pm) The former home of Mewar's rulers, it actually consists of four major and several minor palaces forming a single breath-taking facade overlooking the lake, topped with an exuberance of domes, arches, cupolas, turrets and crenellations.

Entrance to the palace is through the **Hathi Pol** (Elephant Gate), leading to the marble **Tripolia** ("triple") gate. Past here, the **Bada Chowk** ("Big Square") is where the ruler's elephants, infantry, cavalry and artillery were massed for inspection before battle.

Continue through Toran Pol, then climb the steps on the far side to reach the **Raj Angan**. Past here, steps continue up past the small **Shrine of Dhuni Mata**, the oldest part of the City Palace, to reach the idyllic **Bada Mahal**, a pillared courtyard garden standing some 27 metres (90ft) above the base of the palace.

Further steps lead back down through the **Dil Kushal Mahal**, strikingly decorated with dozens of paintings showing scenes from courtly life, and the adjacent **Kanch ki Burj**, covered in brilliant mirrorwork. Further down is the exquisite **Mor Chowk**, decorated with three intricately crafted mosaic peacocks.

Manek Mahal

Hotel in Fateh Prakash Palace

Nearby **Bhim Vilas** is home to a famous sun window, the so-called **Suraj Gokhala**.

Manek Mahal (Ruby Palace) is another of the palace's many superbly mirrored rooms, this time dressed in opulent reds and greens. Past here, a long, twisting corridor winds onwards into **Zenana Mahal** (Palace of the Queens), now home to displays of assorted heirlooms and state treasures. From here, the route continues to **Laxmi Chowk** courtyard, flanked by the queen's domed apartments and centred on a pavilion embellished with a magnificent fretwork peacock.

Exit the main part of the City Palace complex and head around the back to the **Fateh Prakash Palace** section of the palace (now a hotel). Here you'll find the cavernous, time-warped **Durbar Hall,** built in the early 1910s and scarcely changed since, with vast chandeliers, creaking furniture and walls covered in dusty portraits. Overlooking the Durbar Hall, the **Crystal Gallery** (daily 9am–7pm) displays an outlandish selection of items fashioned from pure crystal made for Sajjan Singh during the 1880s, including a solid-crystal bed.

The old city

Close by the main gate of the City Palace is the striking **Jagdish Temple C**, built in 1651 and dedicated to Jagannath, an aspect of Lord Vishnu, with a heavily carved central shrine and an enormous black stone image of Jagannath inside. Nearby, **Bagore-ki-Haveli D** is an elegant 18th-century lakeside mansion now converted into a rewarding museum and performing arts centre, hosting good traditional music and dance shows nightly at 7pm. The **museum** (daily 9.30am–5.30pm) features a number of rooms with meticulously recreated period interiors.

Stretching away east of the City Palace are the Udaipur's main bazaars. Running northeast from the clocktower, **Bara Bazaar E** is the city's top spot for jewellery, with dozens of shops filled with delicate silver bracelets, necklaces and earrings. A little further north is the centre for Rajasthan's traditional culture, the **Bharatiya Lok Kala F**. The centre's **museum** (daily 9am–5.30pm) houses interesting exhibits on local music and dances and also stages short puppet shows on request (donation) plus regular music and dance shows at 7pm.

Octopussy

Sajjan Garh was one of several locations around Udaipur used in the 1983 James Bond film *Octopussy*, where it served as the lair of arch-villain Kamal Khan. The film is still regularly shown in cafés around town, and the high-speed auto-rickshaw chase through the old city still raises a laugh, even today.

AROUND UDAIPUR

Some 5km (3 miles) west of Udaipur, and visible from miles around, is **Sajjan Garh Palace**, or the 'Monsoon Palace', as it's popularly known. Constructed in the late 18th-century, the building stands 750 metres (2,468ft) above sea level, offering breath-taking views.

Rising around a tank some 2km (1 mile) east of the old city, the 19 white marble cenotaphs at **Ahar** mark the cremation site of the former kings of Mewar, as well as the site at which the deceased rulers' queens committed *sati* following their husbands' deaths.

On the south side of Fateh Sagar lake, around 4km (2.5 miles) from the city centre, the 'crafts village' of **Shilpgram** (www.shilpgram.in; daily 11am–7pm) provides an interesting – if rather contrived – window into traditional Rajasthani arts,

View from Monsoon Palace

crafts and vernacular architecture, with 30-odd traditional buildings from five different states in western India, including some Rajasthani-style dwellings brightly painted in colourful murals. Musicians, puppeteers and dancers also hang out around the village, along with various artisans.

NORTH OF UDAIPUR

Some 22km (14 miles) north of Udaipur, **Kailashpuri** village is home to a remarkable complex of 108 temples surrounded by a high fortified wall and centred on the 15th-century **Sri Eklingji Temple**. Built of granite and marble, the shrine has a large, ornate *mandapa* (pillared hall) under a huge pyramidal roof, with a four-faced black marble image of Shiva in the inner sanctuary.

Close to Kailashpuri, **Nagda** is home to an interesting pair of ancient temples known as **Sas-Bahu** and **Adbhutji**. *Sas-Bahu* (meaning 'mother-in-law and daughter-in-law') dates back to the 11th century and is famed for its beautiful carvings, while Adbhutji is an old Jain temple named after a somewhat odd statue of a Jain saint seated within. *Adbhut* means, quite literally, 'peculiar'.

Further north, past Sri Eklingji, the town of **Nathdwara** ㉒ ('Door of God') is one of the Rajasthan's principal pilgrimage destinations, home to the ever popular **Sri Nathdji Temple** – look for the beautiful *pichwais* (devotional paintings showing scenes from the life of Krishna*)* in the inner shrine. The town itself is also full of colour and interest, with narrow cobbled streets winding up the hill to the temple lined with little shops selling all manner of religious trinkets and souvenirs.

KUMBHALGARH

Some 65km (40 miles) from Udaipur, **Kumbhalgarh** ㉓ (daily 9am–5pm) was once the second most important fortress in Mewar after Chittorgarh, built in the mid-15th century to defend the border

Kubulgarh ramparts

Kumbulgarh's huge crenellated ramparts stretch for over 38km (26 miles) across the wild and thickly wooded surrounding hillsides and are claimed to form the world's second-longest wall, beaten only by the Great Wall of China.

between the Rajput kingdoms of Mewar (Udaipur) and Marwar (Jodhpur). Sitting on top of a rocky peak of the Aravalli Mountains, 1,100 metres (3,500ft) above sea level, the fort's inaccessibility made it a safe refuge in times of strife and it fell only once, to the armies of Emperor Akbar.

The vast bastions enclose a huge swathe of land complete with houses, temples, fields and wells – everything needed to withstand a long siege. Most visitors see only a tiny fraction of the entire fort, around the main **Ram Pol** gate, with buildings here including the surprisingly plain palace itself along with various Hindu and Jain temples and assorted cenotaphs, including that of the fort's creator, legendary Rajput ruler Rana Kumbha, just to the east.

RANAKPUR

Nestled in a wooded valley deep in the Aravallis some 100km (60 miles) north of Udaipur, the Jain temples of **Ranakpur** ❷ are amongst India's most exquisite religious monuments. At the centre of the temple complex is the magnificent **Chaumukha** ("four-faced"; daily noon–5pm; free), dedicated to Adinath, the first Jain *tirthankara* (revealer of truth, or literally, 'ford maker'). One of the largest and most complex of all Indian Jain temples, the Chaumukha is encircled by lofty boundary walls and built on a high plinth, with five towers rising above the shrines within. Three entrances lead through columned courts into the main halls – a dazzling design of *mandapas* and courtyards spreading over 3,600 sq metres (40,000 sq ft). The 29 halls containing a staggering 1,444 pillars, each individually carved with a own unique set of astonishingly intricate designs, centred on a 100-pillared shrine housing a white marble image of Chaumukha himself.

A further trio of temples can be found nearby, including two further Jain shrines, built in the 14th century and dedicated to the *tirthankaras* Neminathji and Paraswakathji, and a more modern polygonal Hindu temple dedicated to the sun god Surya, embellished with a running band of solar deities seated in racing chariots.

MOUNT ABU

In the far southwestern corner of the state, the broken ridges of the Aravalli Mountains reach their highest point (1,722

Aravalli Hills, Ajmer

metres/5,649ft) at **Guru Shikhar**, the Saints' Pinnacle, close to the state border with Gujarat. Tucked away in the tangled topography of peaks and valleys below is the diminutive hill station of **Mount Abu ㉕**, an enduringly popular destination with local holiday-makers and, especially, honeymooners.

A stand-out attraction of this area are the spectacular **Dilwara Jain Temples, located** around 3km (2 miles), north of Mount Abu (daily noon–6pm; donation), rivalling those at Ranakpur to the north for the incredible intricacy of their architecture and carvings. The older of the two main temples, the **Vimal Vasahi**, dates from 1031. Dedicated to Adinath, the temple is plain on the outside but a riot of sculptural invention within, topped by a marble dome supported by an intricate design of richly detailed columns carved with dancers,

Toad Rock, Mount Abu

musicians and assorted animals. Beyond, the inner sanctum, enclosed within a covered cloister, protects an image of a meditating Adinath. Outside, the unusual **Hathisala** (Elephant Room) comprises a long hall inhabited by ten beautifully carved and strikingly realistic marble elephants.

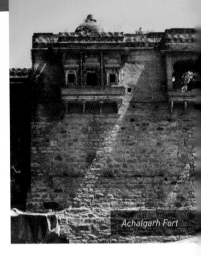
Achalgarh Fort

Close by, the **Luna Vasahi** (dedicated to the 22nd *tirthankara*, Neminath) was built in 1230 and also boasts a staggering profusion of marble work on its convoluted scroll arches and covered pillars, with no two alike. The elaborate scenes carved in bas-relief on the corridor ceilings and the stalactite-like pendant in the main central dome are well worth seeing.

There are many beautiful walks through the hills around town including up to the popular Sunset Point southwest of Nakki Lake. Further afield, there are interesting excursions to the ruins of **Achalgarh Fort**, 8km (5 miles) away and nearby temples, and to **Gaumukh Temple** (literally the 'cow's mouth'), 7km (4 miles) from Mount Abu. The latter marks the scene of the ancient *agnikund* (fire ceremony), from which the Rajput clans are said to have sprung. A natural spring flows out of a carved cow's mouth outside the temple, with pilgrims taking bottles of the precious holy water home with them as a memento of their visit.

Panera Bar at Shiv Niwas Palace

WHAT TO DO

NIGHTLIFE AND DRINKING

Rajasthan is fairly sleepy after dark, and there's very little in the way of Western-style nightlife. Places to drink are fairly thin on the ground (and non-existent outside the major cities), although it's well worth a visit to one of the lavish colonial-era bars located inside the opulent palaces of the former majarajas. For a peek inside Rajasthan's most spectacular royal residence, head to the gorgeous colonial-style **Trophy Bar** at the monumental Umaid Bhawan Palace in Jodhpur (tel: 0291 251 0101, www.taj.tajhotels.com). In Jaipur, the place to go is the quirky **Steam Bar** at the landmark Rambagh Palace Hotel (tel: 0141 238 5700, www.taj.tajhotels.com), located, improbably, inside a beautiful colonial-era steam train and attached miniature railway station. In Udaipur, the enjoyably time-warped **Panera Bar** in the historic Shiv Niwas Palace (tel: 0294 252 8016) also has heaps of colonial-era atmosphere, complete with plush sofas, antique bric-a-brac and huge chandeliers.

MUSIC, DANCE AND PUPPETRY

Rajasthan has a rich tradition of music, dance and puppetry, traditionally staged by castes of hereditary performers (both Hindu and Muslim) during local fairs, festivals, weddings and temple ceremonies, although there are also various places hosting regular shows to cater to the tourist market. In Udaipur, the **Bharatiya Lok Kala Mandal** (Chetak Circle, tel: 0294 252 5077) stages folk dances and puppet shows every evening, while the nearby **Bagore-ki-Haveli** (Gangaur Ghat, tel: 0294 1220 0345) hosts excellent nightly dance performances. In Jaipur, the place to head for is the hugely popular **Chokhi Dhani** "cultural village" (tel: 0141 516 5000, www.chokhidhani.com), some 22 km (14 miles) south of town on the Tonk Road, with nightly folk dances, music, puppetry, acrobatics and magicians, plus attached Rajasthani restaurant serving excellent authentic local food. Less traditional but still great fun are performances by celebrated Rajasthani drag artist **Queen Harish** (Suthar Para, Jaisalmer, tel: 094 1414 9115, www.queenharish.com), the "dancing, whirling desert queen", who performs spectacular folk-dancing shows in the desert near Jaisalmer, when in town.

SHOPPING

Shopping for the state's varied and uniquely colourful handicrafts is one of the major pleasures of a visit to Rajasthan.

⊙ CINEMA

Cinema is massively popular in India – over 2 billion tickets were sold in 2016, almost twice as many as any other country in the world – while top Bollywood stars enjoy almost god-like status. The country is also the world's most prolific producer of films, with as many as two thousand flicks made every year, not only in the Bollywood studios of Mumbai but also in other cities including Chennai ('Kollywood') and Kolkata ('Tollywood'). Cinema buffs shouldn't miss visiting Jaipur's spectacular Art Deco Raj Mandir Cinema (Bhagwan Das Road, off M.I. Road, tel: 0141 237 4694, www.theraj-mandir.com), a major landmark in the city and a great place to enjoy a night of blockbuster Bollywood action.

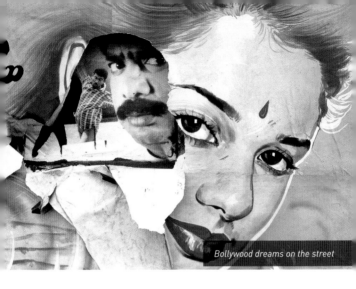

Bollywood dreams on the street

Jaipur is the main centre, while Jodhpur, Jaisalmer and Udaipur are also crammed with shops, and indeed you'll find interesting crafts at outlets all over the state. It's also well worth visiting one or more of the artisan villages in which these crafts originate – the block-printing villages of Sanganer and Bagru, near Jaipur, are particularly rewarding.

Good collectibles include all sorts of textiles (block-printed, tie-dyed, embroidered and so on), jewellery (particularly silver jewellery, and traditional *meenakari* work – silver or gold with enamel inlay), gems (beware scams abound – only buy from reputable outlets), colourful lac bangles, leatherware (including, particularly around Jaisalmer, bags and shoes made form camel hide), puppets, miniature paintings and traditional leather slippers including *jutis* with their distinctive turned-up toes, and *mojadis* – soft slippers embroidered with bright colours.

Indian tailors are very skilful and can run up a set of clothes quickly. Although they can do fair copies of Western fashions, they are, obviously, much better at stitching sari blouses or *shalwar kamiz*. Tailors will also be able to repair your existing clothes, even badly torn ones, and – just as useful – can repair rucksacks which are on the point of collapse and replace zips.

In many large towns, branches of the Rajasthan Government-operated **Rajasthali** chain (www.rajasthali. gov.in) sell a wide range of local handicrafts at fixed prices. Elsewhere, be aware that haggling is accepted – indeed almost expected – in most shops apart from government handicrafts emporia. Note too that the purchase and export of ivory in any form and items made from wild animal products is banned.

JAIPUR

Jaipur is a positive hive of artisanal activity and the undoubted epicentre of the state's craft traditions, with everything for sale from exquisite textiles and delicate bangles through to life-sized marble statues of Hindu gods and godesses. The city is also known for its 'blue pottery', with hand-painted items decorated with floral motifs and geometric patterns in combinations of blue and white (and occasionally other colours).

One word of warning: Jaipur is notorious for its gemstone scams, with tourists being told that they can buy gems in the city and then re-sell them back home at a substantial profit – though you'll most likely end up with a worthless pile of cut-glass baubles and a hefty credit card bill (never let your card out of sight if paying this way).

The biggest name in Rajasthani textiles and clothing, **Anokhi** (KK Square Mall, Prithviraj Rd, C-Scheme, tel: 0141 400 7244, www.anokhi.com) sells quality, fair-trade clothes and homeware in traditional block-printed designs. They also have shops in Jodhpur and Udaipur. Similar to Anokhi, **Soma** (Soma House, Khatipura, tel: 0141 235 2391, www.somashop.com), has attractive clothes and homeware in traditional Indian designs. **Ratan Textiles** (Ajmer Road, tel: 0141 408 0444, www.ratanjaipur.com) offers a good range of hand-block printed textiles, clothes and accessories, while **Kilol** (Sardar Patel Marg, C-Scheme, tel: 0141 222 1343, https://kilol.com) produces quality hand-block printed *dupattas*, *kurtas*, saris and fabrics. For gorgeous cashmere and pashmina clothes and homeware, **Heritage Textiles and Handicrafts** (10 Gangapole Rd, tel: 098 2956 0549, www.heritagetextiles.com) is the place to go, while there are great and very affordable local fashions at **Cottons** (Kalyan Kunj, Civil Lines, tel: 0141 403 9811, www.cottonsjaipur.com), a socially responsible clothes shop selling pretty women's and children's garments. **Mojari** (Shiv Heera Path, C-Scheme, tel: 096 4903 2777, www.facebook.com/Mojari.India) is a UN-supported shop selling a wide range of quality shoes in stylish traditional designs. If you want to get your own clothes made up, make a beeline for **Jodhpur Tailors** (Motilal Atal Marg, tel: 099 8332 1984, www.jodhpurtailors.com),

Shopping for fabrics in Jaipur

A pattern on a blue Rajasthani pottery bowl, Jaipur

whose top-notch tailors are used by the maharaja of Jaipur himself.

For blue pottery, the place to go is **Kripal Kumbh** (Shiv Marg, Bani Park, tel: 0141 220 1127, www.kripalkumbh.com), which has an excellent selection of pieces produced in the former workshop of the late Kripal Singh, the pioneering artist who single-handedly revived the art in Rajasthan. One of the numerous upmarket boutiques along M.I. Road, **The Gem Palace** (M.I. Road, tel: 098 2934 0722, www. munnuthegempalacejaipur.com) is a long-established and reputable jewellers selling beautiful, albeit expensive, creations.

JODHPUR

The quirky **Lalji Handicrafts** (Umaid Bhawan Palace Rd, tel: 098 2902 5888, www.laljihandicrafts.com) consists of a huge, warehouse-like shop stuffed with all sorts of antique curios, collectibles and bric-a-brac, while **Raju's** (Jaljog Circle, Residency Rd, tel: 0291 263 8894, www.rajusfashionmall.com) offers colourful, top-quality saris and *salwar kameez*. The ever-popular **Mohanlal Verhomal's (MV) Spice Shop** (just west of the clock tower, Sardar Bazaar, tel: 0291 510 9347, www.mvspices.com) has a huge selection of local spices and speciality teas.

JAISALMER

Jaisalmer is a particularly good place to shop for textiles and other collectibles, as well as an excellent range of leather-work made from local camel hides. **Ajay Leather Shop** (Fort Road, Amar Sagar Pol, tel: 096 9430 7055) has good, inexpensive camel leather shoes, bags and other items, while brilliant textiles – including superb antique pieces – can be found at the **Barmer Embroidery House** (near Patwa Haveli, tel: 098 2882 5635). **Shree Laxmi Art Home** (Jaisalmer Fort, near Laxminath Temple, tel: 087 6963 5233, www.shreelaxmiarthome.com) also has a nice range of affordable clothes and textiles, while **Hari Om Jewellers** (Chougen Para, Jaisalmer Fort, tel: 094 1467 1025) produces beautiful hand-crafted jewellery, including superb silver rings.

⊙ CRICKET

Cricket is India's national sporting obsession. The main stadium in Rajasthan is Jaipur's Sawai Mansingh Stadium, which hosts occasional international one-day matches. It's also home to the **Rajasthan Royals** (www.rajasthanroyals.com), one of the most successful teams in the booming Indian Premier Twenty20 League – despite being suspended from the league during the 2016 and 2017 seasons for alleged corruption. The Royals have a reputation for unearthing and nurturing outstanding local cricketing talents but have also recruited some of the biggest names in world cricket. Previous captains have included Shane Warne and Rahul Dravid, while the current squad features the stellar talents of Australian batsman Steve Smith and English players Ben Stokes and Jos Buttler.

UDAIPUR

Udaipur is particularly good for miniature paintings. **Gothwal Art** (20 Gangaur Ghat, tel: 096 8028 0701) has an excellent selection of exquisite traditional miniature paintings and other artworks created on the premises by the artist owners, while **KK Art School** (City Palace Road, tel: 0773 734 0192) is another good place to pick up traditional Mewari-style miniature paintings. **Silver Corner** (15 Lal Ghat, tel: 098 2858 2203) has an excellent selection of quality, affordable silver jewellery.

Painting the picture of Udaipur city with oil colours

CAMEL TREKKING

Rajasthan is perhaps the best place in the world to go camel trekking, and the experience of rolling slowly across the sweeping sands of the Thar Desert on camel-back is often a highlight of many visitors' trip. Jaisalmer is far and away the most popular base, with myriad operators offering treks lasting anything from a day to several weeks. Safaris are offered by myriad tour companies and touts around town, although many places put profit over quality of service, so choosing a good tour operator is key. Camel safaris in the past traditionally stuck to the immediate environs of Jaisalmer, but given the number of tourists now out in the desert, better operators tend to start some distance away from town (as much as 60km/37 miles) in order to provide a quiet and authentic experience. Take a hat, sunscreen and plenty of water, although unfortunately, unless you're a seasoned camel jockey there's not much you can do to avoid ending your trip with stiff legs and a decidedly sore behind. Alternatively, there are also a number of operators arranging trips around Bikaner, venturing into significantly less visited and developed areas of desert.

TREKKING

Traditional trekking on foot comes a distant second in popularity to camel trekking in Rajasthan, although there's

Polo

Jaipur is one of India's major polo centres, and a good place to try your hand at this traditional sport of the maharajas. **The Jaipur Polo and Riding Club** (tel: 0141 402 4884, www.jaipurpolo.com) offers lessons for both novices and more experienced players, and also stages regular matches.

some magnificent hiking territory in the dramatic wooded Aravalli hills. **Hiking & Trekking Company Mount Abu** (tel: 099 8320 4776, www.hikingtrekkingmountabu.com) offer beautiful day-treks in the wild and unspoilt hill country around Mount Abu, while **Rajasthan Trekking** (tel: 0723 286 5205, www.rajasthantrekking.com) organize rewarding one- to seven-day treks in the Aravallis around Udaipur, Ranakpur and Kumbulgarh.

HORSE RIDING

Rajasthan has a long equestrian tradition, and taking to the saddle aboard one of the state's famous thoroughbred Marwari mounts is a great way of seeing the countryside. Two good overseas operator are **In the Saddle** (UK tel: 01299 272997, www.inthesaddle.com), organizing various rides in Shekhawati and elsewhere in Rajasthan, often designed to coincide with major local fairs, and **Unicorn Trails** (tel: 01767 777 109 in the UK, 1-888 478 7658 in North America, www.unicorntrails.com), offering assorted Rajasthani rides, with visits to Pushkar and Nagaur fairs. Good local operators include **Dundlod Horse Safaris** (tel: 01594 252 519, www.dundlod.com) in Shekhawati, and **Princess Trails** in Udaipur (tel: 098 2904 2012, www.princesstrails.com).

CYCLING

Rajasthan Cycling Tours (tel: 072 3286 5205, www.rajasthan-cyclingtours.com) arrange a wide range of cycling tours from one-day excursions around southern Rajasthan to two-week expeditions travelling across the state. **Intrepid Travel** (www. intrepidtravel.com) also operate the highly rated 15-day Cycle Rajasthan tour around the state.

WILDLIFE AND BIRDWATCHING

There are numerous excellent wildlife and birdwatching destinations across Rajasthan. The state boasts two of India's finest national parks – the world-famous **Ranthambore Tiger Reserve** and the birdwatching hotspot of **Keoladeo National Park** at Bharatpur – along with numerous other sanctuaries and reserves, including the slowly reviving **Sariska Tiger Reserve** near Alwar. The world-famous tigers of Ranthambore are without doubt the main draw. Leopards are also occasionally spotted, along with numerous species of deer and antelope, sloth bears, wild boar, hyena, mongooses and crocodiles. You'll see captive

Oriental Darter,
Keoladeo National Park

elephants in a number of places, although sadly Rajasthan no longer has any elephants in the wild.

Birdwatchers head to the superb **Keoladeo National Park** at Bharatpur, one of India's finest birding destinations, while over 300 species have also been recorded at Ranthambore.

Virtually all tour operators include some wildlife element in their Rajasthan packages, and many also offer dedicated wildlife tours. Specialist operators include the highly rated **Nature Trek** (UK tel: 01962 733 051, www.naturetrek.co.uk).

YOGA, MEDITATION AND ASTROLOGY

The ancient Indian spiritual practice of yoga, meditation and astrology are all well represented in Rajasthan. Yoga

Yoga with a view

classes are available for all standards from absolute beginners to experienced students. In Jaipur, **Kaivalyadhama Yoga Centre** (tel: 098 2027 3334, www.kdham.com/jaipur), who run morning and evening Ashtanga yoga classes, while **Yoga Peace** (tel: 094 141 410 1525, www.yogapeace.org) offer a wide range of group and individual yoga and meditation classes. In Udaipur, there are daily morning drop-in classes, plus private lessons at **Ashtang**

Yoga Ashram (tel: 093 5247 7577, www.facebook.com/ash-tangyogaashram.udaipur), while in Pushkar the highly rated **Pushkar Yoga Garden** (tel: 098 2827 9835, www.pushkaryoga-garden.com) offers morning and evening Hatha yoga classes, plus yoga and meditation courses (3–30 days). There are also regular classes in Jodhpur with leading local expert Karan Singh (tel: 0291 251 0209, www.yogagurukaransingh.com).

Serious students of meditation might consider one of the transformative Vipassana meditation retreats (held at Jaipur, Jodhpur, Pushkar and Mount Abu) run by the **Dhamma Thali Vipassana Meditation Centre** (tel: 0141 217 7446, www.thali. dhamma.org).

The world-renowned skills of India's fabled astrologers can also be consulted. Two of the best in Rajasthan are Vinod Shastri (tel: 094 1405 1117, www.vinodshastri.com), one of India's leading astrologers and palmists, based at the **Rajasthan Astrological Council** behind the Jantar Mantar Observatory in Jaipur, and S.L. Sharma (tel: 094 1413 0200, www.slsharmapalmist.com), another leading local astrologer and palmistry expert (don't wear nail varnish to your appointment), based at the Moti Mahal section of Meherangarh Fort in Jodhpur.

AYURVEDA AND MASSAGE

The ancient Indian holistic medical and well-being science of Ayurveda is enjoying a massive revival in modern India. Rajasthan isn't a major Ayurvedic centre, but there are a few good places to try it around the state, along with various massage centres and more mainstream Western-style spas.

In Jaipur, **Kerala Ayurveda Kendra** (32 Indra Colony, Bani Park, tel: 0141 402 2446, www.keralaayurvedakendra.com)

An Ayurvedic panchakarma patient at the Indian Institute for Ayurveda

offers a wide range of massages and Ayurveda treatments, while the **Chakrapani Ayurveda Clinic and Research Centre** (8 Shanti Path, Tulsi Circle, tel: 0141 262 4003, www.chakrapani-ayurveda.com) training institute provides treatments and free consultations. In Pushkar the **Deepak Ayurveda Massage Centre** (Vaam Dev Road, tel: 098 2878 7129, www.deepakayurvedapushkar.com) provides excellent Ayurvedic and traditional Rajasthani massages.

CHILDREN'S ACTIVITIES

Highlights of a visit to Rajasthan for children are undoubtedly the chance to go searching for wild tigers at **Ranthambore National Park** (see p.47), and, for older and more robust kids, a camel trek through the desert around Jaisalmer (see p.96). A bike ride around the beautiful **Keoladeo National Park** (see p.45) in Bharatpur should also appeal, while horse-riding (see p.98) is another guaranteed hit with older kids, and everyone will enjoy a breezy boat trip around the lake at Udaipur. The chance to whizz through the traffic in a local rickshaw is also fun, as is shopping for colourful local souvenirs in any of the state's bazaars.

CALENDAR OF EVENTS

Variable dates: Urs Mela, Ajmer. The largest Islamic festival in Rajasthan, lasting up to six days, featuring mass pilgrimages and performances of traditional *qawali* devotional music. Dates change annually according to the Islamic lunar calendar.

February: Nagaur Fair, Nagaur. Traditional cattle fair where villagers also trade in camels, horses and bullocks.

Desert Festival, Jaisalmer. Including acrobatics, turban-tying displays and some of the biggest camel races you'll ever see.

March: Elephant Festival, Jaipur. A lively festival held during Holi festival with lots of activities including elephant parades, polo and races.

April: Gangaur Festival, Jaipur. Traditional spring festival commemorating the love between Shiva and Parvati.

Summer Festival, Mount Abu. Three-day festival of Rajasthani and Gujarati music and dance.

July/August: Teej Festival, Jaipur. Traditional festival welcoming the monsoon. Local women pattern their hands and feet with henna and buy new bangles and clothes.

September: Ramdevra Fair, near Jaisalmer. A large two-day fair attended by devotees of the saint Baba Ramdev, who flock to his shrine to pay homage.

October: Rajasthan International Folk Festival, Mehrangarh Fort Jodhpur. Music and arts festival showcasing local folk music and other performing arts.

Dussehra Mela, Kota. Two-week festival during which people from all over Rajasthan gather to celebrate the victory of Rama over the 10-headed demon king Ravana.

Marwar Festival, Jodhpur. Music and local dance performed on the night of the full moon.

November: Pushkar Festival and Camel Fair. Thousands of pilgrims flock to the small town of Pushkar for a ritual bathe in the lake. The nearby cattle, horse and camel fair takes place during the preceding four days.

December: Winter Festival, Mount Abu. A three-day festival, with Rajasthani and Gujarati music and dance.

EATING OUT

Rajasthani cuisine has been strongly influenced both by the varied lifestyles of its inhabitants and the availability of ingredients in this arid region, where food, fuel and water are all often in scarce supply. Rajasthanis have traditionally favoured non-perishable foods which could be eaten without heating, while milk and ghee were often used instead of water. The lack of green vegetables was compensated for by the extensive use of dried pulses alongisde common local plants like *sangri* (the pods of the ubiquitous khejri tree) and the caper-like berry of the *ker* tree, the two often combined in the classic *ker sangri*.

The Rajputs are predominantly meat-eaters – meat being

Gatte Ka Pulao

thought essential to maintain fighting prowess among the ruling *kshatriya* (warrior) class. Game meat was popular, reflecting the Rajput love of hunting, giving birth to classic dishes such as the spicy *laal maas*. By contrast, many non-Rajputs living in the state, including Jains and Marwaris, were strictly vegetarian – the latter introduced the concept of the *Marwari Bhojnalaya*, the no-frills cafés serving thali-style pure-veg meals, now found across India.

Rajasthan's signature dish is *dhal bati churma*, made of *bati* (baked wheat-flour balls with a distinctively hard crust) plus *churma* (a sweet made of coarsely ground wheat flour mixed with ghee and sugar) and *dhal*. The three are served together thali-style, sometimes accompanied by other vegetable curries.

Gatta, small dumplings of gram flour (made from ground chickpeas) feature in many classic Rajasthani

recipes. These include the biryani-like *gatta ka pulao* and *gatta ki khichdi*, the healthy *gatta ki sabji* (*ghatta* cooked with vegetables) or, best of all, *govind gatta*, featuring large *gatta* stuffed with nuts and served in a thick sauce. *Mangodi* is another popular type of dumpling, made from lentil-flour and usually served in a curry with ingredients which might include potatoes (*alu mangodi*), onions (*mangodi piaza*) or fenugreek (*methi mangodi*). *Khichri* (or *khichdi*) is another popular local vegetarian dish, a thick, warming dahl of almost porridge-like consistency made from lentils, flavoured with a pinch of ghee and spices.

The signature Rajasthani meat dish is *lal maas* (also spellt *laal maans*, meaning 'red meat'), a spicy dish of meat marinated in chilli whose feisty flavours and wine-dark sauce offer a culinary emblem of region's red-blooded, meat-loving Rajput warriors. A favourite amongst the region's ruling classes, *lal maas* was traditionally made using using wild game such as boar or deer,

Jungli Laal Maas spicy hot lamb meat curry from Jaipur

although nowadays it's more likely to be lamb or mutton. Typical accompaniments include chapattis made of wheat or *bajra* millet, the latter grown locally and traditionally eaten during the winter months. *Safed maas* ('white meat') is similar but noticeably cooler, with the meat cooked in a mild cashew, curd and cream gravy. *Sula* is Rajasthani-style tandoori kebab cooked in a distinctively sour and tangy marinade using *kachri*, another local vegetable halfway between a melon and a cucumber.

As throughout India, spicy street snacks and sticky sweets are popular everywhere. Many are made with *mawa*, milk that's been boiled down until it solidifies. Classic taste-bud teasers range from *mawa kachori* (*kachori – a kind of puffed-up flour ball – filled with mawa and drizzled with syrup*) through to *mirchi vada*, a single large deep-fried chilli – approach with caution.

Local specialities aside, the classic dishes of North India dominate most menus. The signature Mughlai-style dishes of nearby Delhi and Agra are widely available, including rich kormas, cooked in mild creamy sauces, sometimes with nuts, fruit and saffron, plus kebabs and biryanis. Punjabi-style meat dishes are also popular including tandooris and tikkas (pieces of meat marinaded in yoghurt and spices, and then roasted in a special tandoori oven). Another Punjabi classic, the delicious murg makhani (butter chicken) also frequently crops up on local menus.

Numerous South Indian restaurants can also be found dotted around all the major cities (particularly Jaipur). Quite different from the cuisine of North India, southern dishes are mainly meat-free, consisting of various types of rice cakes and pancakes. Pride of place goes to the ubiquitous *dosa*, a large rice pancake, most commonly served with a filling of spicy potato curry as a *masala dosa*. Other typical offerings include *uttampam*, a thicker type of rice pancake eaten with a helping of veg curry on the side, and *idlis*, steamed rice cakes served with curry or dhal. Vegetarian versions of all these dishes are also widely available, with paneer (cottage cheese) often serving as a delicious meat substitute.

WHERE TO EAT

Good food can be found in many hotel and guesthouse restaurants. Most hotel restaurants are open for lunch and dinner, usually from around noon to 3pm, and then from 6pm to 10.30pm. Booking is not usually necessary except in particularly

BOOK IN ADVANCE

Restaurant reservations are usually a good idea in upmarket dining venues, particularly in hotel restaurants, but aren't generally needed elsewhere. Cheaper places often don't accept reservations in any case, and if they're full you'll just have to wait until a table becomes free.

upmarket places (particularly in hotels), where it's usually a good idea to phone ahead to make a reservation. Most places serve up a fairly generic selection of traditional North Indian favourites such as *sag panir*, various *kormas*, chicken dishes and *tandoori* breads. Tracking down good, authentic local Rajasthani food is more difficult. Indianised versions of Chinese food such as 'chilli chicken' and simple 'continental' meals catering to the mass-tourist market are also widely available, while Western-style fast food, breads and cakes are also now becoming increasingly prevalent in the larger cities and tourist hotspots.

DRINKS

The classic Indian drink is chai, Indian-style tea, served in local cafes and by pavement vendors just about everywhere

⊙ CHEAP EATS IN RAJASTHAN

If you want to eat like a local at rock-bottom prices, head to one of the state's myriad simple, small and cheap eating places (generally open all day) often known as *bhojanalyas* in Rajasthan (or *dhabas* in the rest of India), or sometimes 'hotels' (even though they have no accommodation). Food hygiene isn't always particularly good, however, with grubby dining rooms and perhaps an even grubbier kitchen, so make sure that the food served to you is freshly cooked and stick to places that look busy. There's also plenty of good street food including snacks ranging from *channa dal* and *puris* to omelettes laden with green chillies and freshly cooked *paratha*. As with most things, use your common sense and only buy from stalls that appear hygienic.

Masala chai in Jaipur

across the state. Chai is made by boiling up water, milk, sugar and spices all together into a drink which is at once strong, sweet and delicately flavoured, combining into a beverage which is surprisingly refreshing in the subcontinental heat. Coffee is less widely available and often of poor quality. Alcoholic drinks are relatively harder to come by (and are banned entirely in the sacred town of Pushkar) and available only in more upmarket or tourist oriented restaurants and cafes, or from local liquor shops. The exorbitant cost of official liquor licences is a major factor in the scarcity of booze, although some guesthouse and café owners serve beer clandestinely without a licence – don't be surprised if you're served your beer in a tea pot. There are also regular "dry days" (usually coinciding with festivals, national/local holidays and elections) when the sale of alcohol is prohibited.

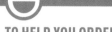
TO HELP YOU ORDER...

I want (a thali) Mujhe (thali) chahiye

Without chilli Mirch ke bina

Little chilli Kam mirch

Hot Garam

Cold Tanda

Ripe/cooked Pukka

Unripe/raw Kucha

AND READ THE MENU....

Mirch Chilli

Namak Salt

Ghee Clarified butter

Dahi Yoghurt

Raita Yoghurt with cucumber

Chawal Rice

Paneer Cheese

Pani Water

Dudh Milk

Lassi Yoghurt drink

Nimbu pani Lime water

Tandur Oven

Pulao Rice made with ghee (clarified butter), spices and vegetables

Biryani Rice cooked with vegetables or meat

Mithai Sweets

Baingain/brinjal Aubergine

Dal Dried pulses

Aum Mango

LOCAL SPECIALITIES

Chappati/roti Unleavened bread made of wheat, barley, millet or maize

Pulao Rice made with ghee (clarified butter), spices and vegetables

Biryani Rice slowly cooked in a clay pot with meat and spices

Bati A baked ball of wheat bread covered with a generous portion of ghee

Masala bati A bati stuffed with peas, dried fruit, spices and mawa

Bajre ki roti Millet roti

Makki ki roti Cornmeal roti

Puri Deep-fried bread

PLACES TO EAT

We have used the following symbols to give an idea of the price of a three course meal for one, excluding drinks.

$$$ Over Rs.2000
$$ Rs.750–2000
$ Under Rs.750

AJMER

Ambrosia $$ *Ashok Marg, tel: 0145 242 5095,* http://www.ambassador ajmer.com/ambrosia. Suave modern outdoor rooftop restaurant at the Ambassador Hotel, with seating in romantic curtained pavilions, plus sweeping views of the Aravalli Hills. Pood comprises a good selection of veg and non-veg Indian standards, plus a few Western dishes.

BHARATPUR

Gulmohar $$$ *Old Agra–Achnera Road, tel: 099 8293 5555,* http://www. thebagh.com/. Part of the lovely The Bagh resort just outside town, Gulmohar is one of the best of Bharatpur's somewhat limited dining options. The menu focuses on vegetarian cooking from the Braj (Mathura) area alongside more mainstream subcontinental dishes, served in a pretty dining room.

BIKANER

Chhotu Motu Joshi Sweet Shop $ *Station Road, tel: 0151 252 3827.* This bustling restaurant, with cheap meals served in large portions, is one of the best place in town for thalis and paratha dal breakfasts. The attached sweet shop with its rasmalais and cham chams is also excellent.

Gallops $$ *Opposite Junagarh Fort, tel: 0151 320 0833.* In a superb location directly opposite the fort, this place is touristy and a bit overpriced but ticks the right boxes food-wise, with good North Indian meat and veg mains including an above-average selection of Rajasthani specialities. Nicest in the evening, when it's less likely to be overrun by coach parties.

BUNDI

Lake View Garden Restaurant $ *Nawal Sager Lake, tel: 092 1466 7453.* This basic guesthouse garden restaurant with plastic chairs won't win any design awards, but the lake views are beautiful and the home-cooked food good and authentic, with tasty Rajasthani thalis and other curries, plus assorted Western light meals.

JAIPUR

Baluchi $$$ *The Lalit, Jagatpura Road, tel: 0141 519 7777,* https://www. thelalit.com/the-lalit-jaipur/eat-and-drink/baluchi/. In the opulent Lalit hotel, this suave modern restaurant serves up some of Rajasthan's best contemporary Indian fine-dining. Dishes feature specialities from across the country, featuring Rajasthani classics like *lal maas* and *dal bati churma* alongside a wide range of unusual dishes from across India. Reserve ahead.

Handi $$ *M.I. Road, tel: 0141 491 7115,* http://www.handirestaurant.com/. Long-running and deservedly popular restaurant with enjoyably rustic décor and a great selection of hearty meat tandooris, tikkas and ke-babs, plus local specialities including spicy Rajasthani *gatta* and a good Jaisalmer-style *laal maas*.

Four Seasons $$ *Subhash Marg, C-Scheme, tel: 0141 237 5221.* Locals rate this place one of the best veg restaurants in town, with excellent North Indian classics served in a comfortably old-school dining room. There are also plenty of South Indian and some European and Chinese options.

Ganesh Restaurant $ *Nehru Bazaar, next to Punjab Tailors, tel: 098 8715 4000.* Hidden away above the shops of Nehru Bazaar, this spit-and-saw-dust *dhaba* offers an enjoyable slice of local life (although it's now firmly on the tourist radar) and decent no-frills food in one of the Pink City's most atmospheric settings.

Peacock Rooftop Restaurant $ *Pearl Palace Hotel, Hari Kishan Somani Marg, tel: 0141 237 3700.* This pretty little restaurant on the roof of the Pearl Palace Hotel caters to a largely tourist crowd and so isn't the most authentic experience you'll have in Jaipur, although the excellent, flavoursome Indian food is as good as any in town, and the international dishes are pretty decent too. Given the quality, prices are a steal.

Shreenath Lassiwala $ *312 M.I. Road, tel: 093 1451 7382.* Famous little shop selling some of the best lassis in the country – sinfully rich and creamy concoctions served in traditional clay mugs. Several copy-cat shops have set up alongside: check the street number (312) to make sure you're at the right place. Usually closes mid-afternoon when the lassi runs out.

Suvarna Mahal $$$ *Rambagh Palace Hotel, Bhawani Singh Road, tel: 0141 238 5700,* https://bit.ly/2nfsMMO. For the ultimate Jaipur night out, nothing beats a trip to the stunning Rambagh Palace. Start with a drink at the atmospheric Steam or Polo bars, then head to Suvarna Mahal, occupying a gloriously time-warped neoclassical dining room and serving up superb Indian cuisine including lavish thalis and richly roasted meats. Reservations essential for non-guests.

JAISALMER

Chandan Shree Restaurant $$ *Next to the taxi stand.* Super-popular local restaurant serving a range of Indian meals – including South Indian dishes and Rajasthani specialities – at rock bottom prices.

Dhanraj Ranmal Bhatia Sweets $ *Bhatia Market, tel: 041 414 9552.* This sweet shop is famous in Jaisalmer and beyond, creating some of the best traditional sweets in the state – their *ladoos* are divine.

Free Tibet $ *Fort Road, tel: 097 8209 4554.* Tucked away in shoebox-sized premises inside the Fort, this place has memorable city views, super-friendly service and a tasty range of international fare plus great Tibetan specialities including the café's signature *momos* (dumplings).

Gaj's Restaurant $ *Kalakar Colony, tel: 098 2903 0701.* Gaj's consistently good Indian, international and – rather unexpectedly – Korean food get rave reviews, backed up by friendly service and fine views over town from the outdoor terrace seats.

The Lal Garh $$ *Patwa Haveli Road, tel: 094 1415 0150.* Attractive rooftop restaurant offering picture-perfect views of Jaisalmer Fort backed up by attentive service and some of the best Indian food in town, affordably priced.

Natraj $ *Aasani Road, tel: 088 9011 1597.* A long-running stalwart of the Jaisalmer tourist scene, this pleasant roof-top establishment serves up decent Indian and Chinese food, with a good selection of veg and, particularly non-veg North Indian curries.

Pleasant Haveli $$ *Gandhi Chowk, tel: 029 9225 3253.* One of the best of all Jaisalmer's innumerable rooftop restaurants, with sweeping views of town, fort and desert from its stylish sandstone terrace – beautiful after dark, and a great place to chill out over a beer and some quality Indian food including good Rajasthani *thalis*.

JODHPUR

Indique $$$ *Pal Haveli, Sardar Bazaar, tel: 0291 329 3328,* http://palhaveli. com/restaurant.php. Get an eyeful of one of Jodhpur's most memorable views from this romantic rooftop restaurant, directly below the fort (particularly stunning after dark). The veg and non-veg Indian menu is pricey but good, especially for meat eaters (try the *lal maas*), and it's licensed too.

Fort View $ *Govind Hotel, Station Road, tel: 0291 262 2758.* The roof-top restaurant at this popular budget guesthouse has nice fort views and dishes up great, inexpensive local food including delicious lassis and a selection of traditional Rajasthani specialities which rarely find their way onto restaurant menus elsewhere.

Gypsy $$ *C Road, Sardarpura, tel: 074 1207 4071* , http://www.gypsyfoods. com/menu.html. Head to the upstairs restaurant for a taste of the famous Gypsy vegetarian Rajasthani thali, which features 30-odd dishes on an average day, including local specialities like *ker sangri* and *dal batti churma*. A fixed price gets you all you can eat, with roving waiters constantly refilling your metal plate until you cry enough.

Shri Mishrilal $ *Sardar Bazaar, tel: 098 2905 8782*. Tucked away inside the southern gateway leading into Sardar Bazaar, this hole-in-the-wall (or, rather, gate) establishment is famous for its superb *makhania* lassi, a thick and sumptuous version of the ubiquitous yogurt-based drink made using a rich combination of saffron, cardamom and cream.

Umaid Bhawan $$$ *Circuit House Road, tel: 0291 251 0101*, https://bit.ly/1W4Rqxr. Rajasthan's most spectacular hotel has two dining options. The signature Risala restaurant serves up a mix of Indian and continental fusion cuisine based on royal recipes, while the less formal Pillars terrace restaurant offers views of the palace's lush garden and a multi-cuisine menu of drinks and light meals. Advance reservations essential.

KOTA

Aarogan $$$ *Umed Bhavan Palace, Palace Road, tel: 0744 232 5262*. Classy restaurant set in the atmospheric old Umed Bhavan Palace hotel and serving up good Indian cuisine alongside some Western dishes. Relax with a drink before or after in the elegant and well-stocked Swinton's Bar.

MOUNT ABU

Jodhpur Bhojnalaya $$ *Near the taxi stand, tel: 094 1415 2295*. This place is the real deal, serving delicious, authentic Rajasthani vegetarian food immersed in *ghee* and spices. If you only eat the classic Rajasthani *dal batti churma* once during your visit, this is the place to have it.

PUSHKAR

Café Nature's Blessing $$ *Panch Kund Road, tel: 096 4962 5538*. One of the best of Pushkar's numerous healthfood-style cafés, serving up a flavour-packed selection of inventive vegetarian dishes – all lovingly prepared from scratch using fresh ingredients and as little oil as possible.

Honeydew Café $ *Main Bazaar, tel: 094 6078 9699*. This tiny café is one of Pushkar's old stalwarts, still going strong thanks to its super-friendly atmosphere and good, fresh healthy veg food including great breakfasts and tasty home-style Indian and international mains. Great coffee and chai, too.

Sunset Café $$ *Parikrama Marg, tel: 098 2855 8382*. A popular hangout towards dusk as travellers congregate to enjoy the stunning sunsets over the lake. The typically Pushkar-style international menu features Indian dishes alongside Tibetan *momos*, Mexican tacos and assorted Italian and continental mains.

The Sixth Sense $$ *Inn Seventh Heaven, Chotti Basti, tel: 0145 510 5455*. In the lovely Seventh Heaven boutique hotel, this suave restaurant offers a distinct change of scenery from the homespun hippy cafés which make up the bulk of Pushkar's eating options, serving up quality Indian and Continental food at surprisingly affordable prices.

SHEKHAWATI

Bungli Restaurant $$, *Kothi Road, Nawalgarh, tel: 076 6571 1416*. Friendly and cosy family restaurant serving up a real taste of authentic Indian home-cooking, with subcontinental classics alongside local specialities, all cooked freshly to order.

Shekhawati Restaurant $$ *Hotel Shekhawati, Mukundgarh Road, Mandawa, tel: 093 1469 8079*. This pleasant hotel is a good place for reliable, tasty and inexpensive Indian food, served up in a colourfully frescoed restaurant with fine views over town towards Mandawa Fort.

UDAIPUR

Ambrai $$$ *Amet Haveli, Chandpole, tel: 0294 243 1589*. One of Udaipur's most romantic restaurants, in a wonderful lakeside location opposite Lal Ghat, with superb City Palace views backed up by excellent Indian food (with the focus on sumptuous tandoori meat dishes), plus live music nightly.

Café Edelweiss $$ *Gangaur Ghat, tel: 094 1423 3571.* The oldest of the myriad "German" bakeries which can now be found across Rajasthan, dishing up freshly made European-style sandwiches, breads, pastries and cakes, plus fresh salads, mueslis and yogurts. Great coffee and other drinks, too.

Hari Garh Restaurant $$ *Hanuman Ghat, tel: 097 7288 0333,* http://www.restaurantharigarh.com. Cosy little lakeside restaurant (with some tables right next to the water) offering a wide-ranging selection of inexpensive and excellently prepared veg and non-veg Indian, continental and Chinese dishes including succulent meat dishes and local Mewari specialities.

Jagat Niwas $$$ *Jagat Niwas Palace Hotel, Lalghat, tel: 0294 242 2860,* http://www.jagatcollection.com/jagatniwas/dining.html. This popular hotel is home to a pair of good restaurants. Choose between the breezy rooftop Chandni (with live puppet shows) or the romantic Jharoka restaurant downstairs, occupying the hotel's beautiful haveli-style courtyard, with live music nightly. The menu features a well prepared selection of both Indian and continental dishes, and there's also a nice little in-house bakery.

Jaiwana Haveli $$ *Lalghat, tel: 0294 252 1252.* Idyllic rooftop restaurant right over the lake, serving reliable Indian, Chinese and continental cuisine including good Rajasthani specialities, although it's the views which really make the place special.

Natraj $ *City Station Road, east of the city centre in the New Bapu Bazaar area, tel: 094 1475 7893.* One of the city's most popular restaurants (and also one of the hardest to find) thanks to its excellent and inexpensive all-you-can eat thalis, pulling in crowds of locals daily. There's also a second, more tourist-oriented branch called Natraj Lodge (behind the Ashok Cinema east of Gangaur Ghat), serving the same food, at slightly higher prices.

Yummy Yoga $$ *Brahmpole Road, tel: 097 8403 9910.* There's good, healthy Indian and European vegetarian food at this welcoming little café – the pumpkin curry gets rave reviews, and they also do good pizza, pasta, good breakfasts and a mean masala chai. Excellent cooking classes, too, if you want to learn a few of their secrets.

A–Z TRAVEL TIPS

A SUMMARY OF PRACTICAL INFORMATION

A

ACCOMMODATION

Accommodation in Rajasthan is extremely varied, ranging from inexpensive homestays through to extravagant royal palaces. At the bottom end of the scale are small local guesthouses, often family run. The best places have a real home-from-home feeling, with friendly hosts offering a window into local life and good home cooking. Smaller local business hotels are also often comfortable and inexpensive places to stay, although usually lacking in much character.

ADMISSION CHARGES

The majority of tourist sites in Rajasthan charge admission fees, although these aren't too punitive, even at major attractions (entry to Jaipur's City Palace, for example, currently costs Rs 400 (around £4.50/$6), while entrance charges at more modest sights may be no more than $0.80/$1 or so – although you'll often have to buy an extra ticket for your camera and/or video, which can bump prices up slightly.

AIRPORTS

There are four passenger airports in Rajasthan: Jaipur International Airport (tel: 0141 255 0623, www.jaipurairport.com), Jodhpur Airport (tel: 0291 251 2934), Udaipur's Maharana Pratap Airport (tel: 0294 265 5950, www.udaipurairport.com), and the recently opened Jaisalmer Airport (tel: 02992 250 048). All four have direct connections with both Delhi and Mumbai, which are the arrival points for most international flights to India.

B

BEGGING

Visitors to Rajasthan will inevitably encounter a fair number of beggars along the way – although these are far less common now than even a decade ago. Beggars particularly congregate around temples, mosques and other shrines, and on railway and bus journeys. Many beggars are physically disabled and they have no way of getting money except by asking for it. It's up to you whether you give or not, of course, although any offering will be gratefully received and even a small sum may make a big difference – but try to give discretely or every other beggar in the vicinity will make a beeline for you. You should, however, avoid giving money to begging children or apparently well-off adults who might simply be chancing their arm in the hope of getting some free cash out of a gullible visitor.

BUDGETING FOR YOUR TRIP

The major cost of visiting Rajasthan is likely to be your plane ticket to India. Flights from the UK to Delhi (your most likely starting point) currently start at around £420 return. From the USA fares begin from roughly $800 from either the east or west coasts.

In Rajasthan itself, a visit can be as cheap or as expensive as you want it to be. Double rooms in budget guesthouses can be had for around Rs 800 (£8/$11) per night or even less, while a room at one of the state's top places can cost approaching £1,000 ($1,300), with many other standards and prices between. Food is generally inexpensive. Cheap main courses in local tourist restaurants usually start from around Rs.200 (£2/$2.75), while five-star hotel restaurants aren't astronomical, and usually a lot cheaper than in the West. Alcohol is relatively expensive, but still not exorbitant: a large bottle of local beer will go for around Rs.200 (£2/$2.75) in a cheap tourist café, although imported wines are pricey.

Transport is extremely good value. The train journey from Delhi to Jaipur, for example, costs as little as Rs 205 (£2/$2.75) in second class reserved, rising to Rs 1295 (£14/$18) in executive A/C chair class on Shatabdi services. Bus fares are similar, although costs can rise sharply if you hire your own car and driver and take domestic flights.

The majority of tourist sites in Rajasthan charge admission fees, although these are relatively modest, even at major attractions (entry to Jaipur's City Palace, for example, currently costs Rs 500 (£5/$7), while entrance charges at smaller sights may be no more than £0.75/$1 or so.

C

CLIMATE

Rajasthan is predominantly hot for most of the year, except in a few elevated places like Mount Abu. Rain is infrequent, except during the monsoon.

October to March is the 'cool' season, with average daytime temperatures of between around 20°C and 25°C, although it often rises above 30°C during the hottest part of the day, and falls below 10°C at night. This is the peak tourist season in Rajasthan (November–January in particular), with prices at their highest and pressure on accommodation at its greatest. February is quieter, while March is a good time to visit, although temperatures are beginning to rise as summer approaches.

Summer, from April to June, is sizzlingly hot, with temperatures hovering close to 30°C even at night and regularly topping the 40°C mark during the day, or even higher – in May 2016 the district of Phalodi in the west of the state set a new record for India's highest ever recorded temperature, over 51°C. Given the conditions, travelling during these months is best avoided. Heavier rains may also start falling in June in the lead up to the monsoon, although temperatures remain sky-high.

The monsoon hits Rajasthan from July to Sept – although exactly how much rain will fall in this period is becoming impossible to predict following the increasingly erratic monsoons of recent years. Even at the height of the wet season the state remains significantly drier than most other parts of India, including nearby Delhi. Temperatures fall slightly, but remain in the 30s, or higher, if the rains fail to appear.

CLOTHING

Loose, light clothing is the best way to deal with Rajasthan's high temperatures, along with a hat and sunglasses – cotton is best, since synthetics can irritate the skin in the heat. There's plenty of good cheap clothing available if you need to replenish your wardrobe en route, and wearing locally made clothes can also help you blend in better too. You'll also need a jumper for the sometimes surprisingly chilly desert evenings and nights. Women should avoid sleeveless tops, short skirts or any form of revealing dress, both to avoid sunburn, to minimize the risk of being sexually harrassed and also to avoid causing offence, embarrassment or just downright consternation in conservative rural areas. Locally available shalwar kamiz, a long tunic top worn over loose trousers, are elegant and appropriate, as is a churidar kurta, a long tunic top worn over tight-fitting trousers. India is a generally safe place to travel, but tourists are natural targets for thieves and pickpockets, so keep your valuables in a money belt or a safe (preferably zipped) inside pocket. Avoiding obvious displays of wealth or flashing expensive watches and jewellery is also sensible – in fact it's better to leave these at home.

CRIME AND SAFETY

India is a generally safe place to travel, but tourists are natural targets for thieves and pickpockets, so keep your valuables in a money belt or a safe (preferably zipped) inside pocket. Avoiding obvious displays of wealth or flashing expensive watches and jewellery is also sensible – in fact it's better to leave these at home.

Do not leave belongings unattended, especially on trains and buses, and watch your luggage carefully during loading and unloading. Invest in good strong locks for your bags and if possible leave valuables in a safe at your hotel (even if you don't have one in your room, management may have one at reception). Chaining luggage to the berth on a train, or to your seat on a bus, is another precaution that travelling Indians often take.

Credit card fraud does exist, so make sure that shops and restaurants process your card in front of you. It's also worth keeping a photocopy of your passport and visa, ticket details, insurance policy number and telephone claims number, and some emergency money in a bag or case separate from your other cash and documents. If you are robbed, report the incident immediately to a police station (be patient, this can take hours, and if possible take a local along with you to help navigate the paperwork and language barriers).

CUSTOMS

Arriving, you'll need to fill in a declaration form (usually handed out on the plane); keep the slip in your passport for when you disembark. Prohibited articles include all the usual items – firearms, proscribed drugs, pornography and live plants.

The duty-free allowance for foreign visitors on arrival is 100 cigarettes and 2 litres of wine or alcoholic spirits. There is no limit on the amount of foreign currency you can import, but any sums in excess of $5,000 must be declared on arrival. Note that the export of antiques (over 100 years old) is prohibited, as is the export of wild animal products, including ivory, reptile skins and furs.

D

DISABLED TRAVELLERS

Although disability is common in India, there are very few provisions for wheelchairs or special toilets. The roads are full of potholes and kerbs are often high and without ramps. If you have difficulty walking, it may be hard to negotiate street obstacles, and pavements (where they exist) are often totally covered in parked vehicles or other obstacles. On the other hand, Indians will always be willing to help you in and out of buses or cars, or up stairs. Taxis and rickshaws are cheap and the driver, with a little baksheesh, will probably help. You could also employ a guide who will be prepared to help with obstacles.

Only a small number of upmarket hotels have rooms adapted for those with special needs – and heritage hotels in old buildings may present particular difficulties when is comes to facilities and accessibility. Few buildings have lifts. Public transport is also problematic. Trains are difficult to board for wheelchair users or those with limited mobility, although you may be able to arrange for station staff to help you get on and off –check in advance at the relevant station. Buses and coaches are not accessible.

Operators arranging accessible holidays to India include: www.disabledholidays.com (with a useful list of accessible hotels in Jaipur and other Indian cities), www.disabilitytravel.com and www.2by2holidays.co.uk.

DRIVING AND CAR HIRE

Driving in India is very much for experienced and confident drivers only. Heavily congested roads and chaotic traffic are the norm in the big cities, and while although things are more relaxed out in the countryside you'll still have to deal with a wide variety of hazards you'll probably not have encountered elsewhere, ranging from massively potholed roads through to wandering camels. If you do decide to try driving in India you'll need an international driving licence to hire a car, available from national motoring organisations like the AA.

Given all this, the vast majority of travellers to India opt to hire a car with driver – any decent hotel, guesthouse or local tour operator should be able to arrange this for trips ranging from a few hours to a week or more. Prices vary widely depending on the standard of the car, the qualifications of the driver and where you book it. A non-a/c car hired through a budget guesthouse or local tour agent might cost as little as £20/day, while a luxury a/c car booked through a five-star hotel can easily cost five times as much. Check that your driver speaks English (however basic) and make it clear where you want to go and what you want to do – many drivers earn extra cash from taking tourists to shops or other establishments where they earn commission and regularly attempt to drag tourists into souvenir emporia against their will.

E

ELECTRICITY

The voltage system in India is 220–240V AC, 50 cycles AC. Most sockets are of the three round-pin variety (European appliances with two-round-pin plugs will work in these), but do vary. Take a universal adaptor for British, Irish and Australasian plugs. American and Canadian appliances may need a transformer. Electricity supplies may be irregular, especially during the summer, as demand often outstrips supply.

EMBASSIES AND CONSULATES

In Delhi:
Australian High Commission
Australian Compound, 1-50G Shantipath, Chanakyapuri, New Delhi
Tel: 011-4139 9900
www.india.highcommission.gov.au
British High Commission
Shantipath, Chanakyapuri, New Delhi
Tel: 011-2419 2100
www.gov.uk
Canadian High Commission
7–8 Shantipath, Chanakyapuri, New Delhi (P.O. Box 5207)
Tel: 011-41178 2000
www.canadainternational.gc.ca
Irish Embassy
C17 Malcha Marg, Chanakyapuri, New Delhi
Tel: 011-4940 3200

www.irelandinindia.com
New Zealand High Commission
Sir Edmund Hillary Marg, Chanyakapuri, New Delhi
Tel: 011-4688 3170
www.mfat.govt.nz/en/embassies
South African High Commission
B-18 Vasant Marg, Vasant Vihar, New Delhi
Tel: 011-2614 9411
www.southafricainindia.wordpress.com
US Embassy
Shantipath, Chanakyapuri, New Delhi
Tel: 011-2419 8000

Indian missions abroad:
Australia
High Commission of India
3–5 Moonah Place, Yarralumla, Canberra ACT-2600
Tel: 02-6273 3999
www.hcindia-au.org
Canada
High Commission of India
10 Springfield Road, Ottawa, Ontario KLM 1 C9
Tel: 613-744 3751
www.hciottawa.ca
Great Britain
High Commission of India
India House, Aldwych, London WC2B 4NA
Tel: 020-7836 8484
www.hcilondon.in
US
Embassy of India
2107 Massachusetts Avenue NW, Washington DC 20008
Tel: 202-939 7000
www.indianembassy.org

EMERGENCIES

In early 2016 it was announced that India will be introducing a new emergency number of 112 from 1 January 2017 to cover police, fire and ambulance services (equivalent to the British 999 or the US and Canadian 911, and replacing the current emergency numbers of 100 for the police, 101 for fire, and 102 for ambulances).

In a medical emergency (depending on what the emergency is and where you are) you may find it quicker to make your own way to the nearest hospital using a rickshaw or taxi rather than waiting for an ambulance. Ask your hotel or guesthouse to assist and advise – they may also be able to drive you.

ETIQUETTE

Always remove your shoes before entering someone's house, a temple or a mosque. Stockinged feet are usually permissible. The greeting with folded hands (the namaste, or namaskar) is the standard Indian form of salutation and its use will be appreciated, though men, especially in the cities, will not hesitate to shake hands with you if you are a man. A handshake would even be appreciated as a gesture of special friendliness.

Most Indian women would be taken aback at the informality of interaction between the sexes common in the West and physical contact between men and women is to be avoided. Men should not shake hands with a woman (unless she first offers to).

Avoid taking leather goods of any kind into temples as these can often cause offence. Photography is prohibited inside the inner sanctum of many temples (and throughout some temples). Visitors are usually welcome to look around at their leisure and can sometimes stay during religious rituals. Modest clothing is essential when visiting places of worship. In mosques, women should cover their head and arms and wear long skirts. A small contribution to the temple donation box (hundi) is customary.

In private, visitors are received as honoured guests and your unfamiliarity with Indian ways will be accepted and understood. When eating with your fingers, remember to use only the right hand.

Avoid pointing the soles of your feet towards anyone as this is considered a sign of disrespect. Don't point with your index finger: use either your extended hand or your chin.

F

FESTIVALS

In addition to the many Hindu, Muslim, Christian and Sikh festivals celebrated throughout North India, Rajasthan has many local festivals which combine with traditional fairs.

Variable

Urs Mela, Ajmer. The largest Islamic festival in Rajasthan, lasting up to six days. The entire town is decorated with bunting and thousands of Muslims come together at the Dargah to commemorate the life of Muin-ud-din Chishti, the Sufi saint who died here in 1236. After the worshipping is over there are excellent qawali performances. Dates change annually according to the Islamic lunar calendar.

January

Bikaner Festival, Bikaner. The Kolagat mela and cattle fair is an important annual festival for the desert people, held on the banks of the holy lake, about 45km (28 miles) from Bikaner.

February

Nagaur Fair, Nagaur. This is a traditional cattle fair where villagers also trade in camels, horses and bullocks.

Desert Festival, Jaisalmer. A festival started by Rajasthan Tourism in 1979 to promote local arts, including acrobatics, turban tying displays and some of the best camel races with the desert units of the Border Security Force.

Brij Festival, Bharatpur. For a few days prior to Holi, this traditional festival includes performances of the Raslila, enacting the love story of Krishna and Radha.

Baneshwar Fair, Baneshwar. Situated at the confluence of the Mali and Som rivers about 60km (37 miles) southeast of Dungarpur, this festival offers one of the few opportunities to see a large gathering of Bhil peoples.

March

Elephant Festival, Jaipur. A lively festival held during Holi with lots of activities including elephant parades, polo and races.

April

Gangaur Festival, Jaipur. A traditional spring festival that is celebrated in Jaipur and elsewhere throughout Rajasthan. Mainly celebrated by women who commemorate the love between Shiva and Parvati.

Mewar Festival, Udaipur. Also celebrated at Gangaur and dedicated to Parvati. The women of Udaipur gather to dress the images of Ishar and Gangaur (Shiva and Parvati) that are then carried in procession through the city to Gangaur Ghat at Lake Pichola, and then in boats along the shore.

Summer Festival, Mount Abu. A three-day festival of Rajasthani and Gujarati music and dance.

July–August

Teej Festival, Jaipur. A traditional festival welcoming the monsoon with excitement and colour. Particularly important for women who apply henna patterns to their hands and feet, and buy new bangles and clothes.

Kajli Teej, Bundi. Celebrates Teej on the third day of the month of Bhadra and continues for eight days until Janamastami, which celebrates Lord Krishna's birthday.

September

Ramdevra Fair, near Jaisalmer. A large two-day fair attended by devotees of the saint Baba Ramdev, who flock to his shrine to pay homage. There are night-long devotional performances with bhajans and kirtans sung throughout this period.

October

Rajasthan International Folk Festival, Jodhpur (www.jodhpurriff.org).

Music and arts festival showcasing local folk music and other perform-ing arts, held in the spectacular setting of Jodhpur's Mehrangarh Fort.
Dussehra Mela, Kota. People from all over Rajasthan gather to worship Lord Rama. The festival celebrates the victory of Lord Rama over the 10-headed demon king Ravana. For two weeks the city becomes a large carnival with temporary shops and markets and cultural programmes. On the day of Dussehra itself giant effigies of Ravana and his brothers, stuffed with fireworks, are burnt.
Marwar Festival, Jodhpur. Music and local dance performed on the night of the full moon.

November
Pushkar Festival and Camel Fair. At the full moon during the month of Kartik, thousands of pilgrims flock to the small town of Pushkar for a ritual bathe in the lake. The nearby cattle, horse and camel fair takes place during the preceding four days.
Chandrabhaga Festival, Jhalawar. A large cattle fair on the banks of the River Chandrabhaga. It is considered sacred to bathe in the river on the full moon night that occurs during the fair.

December
Winter Festival, Mount Abu. A three-day festival, with Rajasthani and Gujarati music and dance.

G

GUIDES AND TOURS

There's a plethora of local tour companies in every tourist centre in Rajasthan, while the region's popularity means that it also features on the tours of many overseas-based companies as well. Some leading international tour operators with a particular speciality in India include Audley Travel (www.audleytravel.com), Greaves India (www.greaves-india.com), Indus Tours (www.industours.co.uk), Insider Tours (www.insider-tours.com) and Trans Indus (www.transindus.co.uk). Good local companies include the Jaipur-based India's Invitation (www.indiasinvitation.com) and Cyclin' Jaipur (www.cyclinjaipur.com), offering a range of innovative tours in Jaipur itself and across the state. Elsewhere, Shri Sanwariya Tours in Udaipur (www.shrisanwariyatours.com) is a reliable option for day-trips around the city.

H

HEALTH AND MEDICAL CARE

Good medical care can be hard to come by outside the big cities. In an emergency, good hospitals include the **Fortis Escorts Hospital** in Jaipur (Jawaharlal Nehru Marg, tel: 0141 254 7000, www.fortishealthcare.com), Medipulse Hospital in **Jodhpur** (opposite AIIMS Campus, tel: 0291 274 0740, www.medipulse.in) and the Maa Gayal Hospital in **Udaipur (**Airport Road, tel: 0294 249 4701, www.maagayatrihospital.com). There are also numerous well-equipped pharmacies in the major cities, usually with English-speaking staff. In the major cities you can call 102 for an ambulance in case of emergencies.

No vaccinations are legally required to enter India, although you may need to show proof of a yellow fever inoculation if arriving from an infected area. It is, however, strongly advised that you get inoculations against typhoid and hepatitis A. Other diseases against which vaccinations might be considered, particularly for longer trips, include meningitis, rabies and Japanese B encephalitis. There is no vaccination against Dengue fever, occasionally contracted in India. The only protection is to avoid being bitten.

Water

Tap water is best avoided. Water in the larger cities is technically safe to drink, but may cause stomach upsets for visitors unused to local micro-organisms, while tap water in more remote areas may be contaminated. Bottled water is widely available, inexpensive and generally safe, but always check that the plastic seal is intact – it's not unknown for used bottles to be refilled from the tap and then resold.

Malaria

This moquito-borne disease is serious and potentially fatal and continues to be a major problem in India. Fortunately the incidence of malaria in Rajasthan is very low, to the point that, if this is the only part of India you're visiting, anti-malarial drugs might not be necessary, although it's essential to seek expert medical advice before travelling. Numerous anti-malarial drugs are available including a combination of proguanil (Paludrine) plus chloroquine (Avoclar, Nivaquin), Malarone and doxycyline.

Malaria is transmitted by the Anopheles mosquito, and the best, and only certain, protection against malaria is not to get bitten. Sleep under a mosquito net, cover up in the evenings and use an effective insect repellent such as DEET (diethyltoluamide). Burning mosquito coils, which are easily obtainable in India, is also a good idea.

Symptoms are similar to acute flu (including some or all of fever, shivering, diarrhoea and muscle pains) and an outbreak may come on as much as a year after visiting a malarial area. If malaria is suspected then medical attention should be sought as soon as possible.

Diarrhoea, dysentery and giardia

Traveller's diarrhoea is usually caused by low-level food poisoning and can be avoided with a little care. An upset stomach is often caused by eating too many rich Indian meat dishes (usually cooked with vast amounts of oil and spices) and failing to rest and let your body acclimatise. Drink plenty of fluids, but never drink unboiled or unfiltered water. Avoid ice as this is often made with unboiled water. All food should be cooked and eaten hot. Don't eat salads and always peel fruit.

Dysentery is characterised by diarrhoea accompanied by the presence of mucus and blood in faeces, plus severe stomach cramps, vomiting and possibly fever. It may clear up by itself, but its usual treatment is with 500mg of ciprofloxacin or tetracycline twice daily for five days. Amoebic dysentery has a slower onset and will not clear up on its own. If you suspect you have amoebic dysentery you should seek medical help as it can damage the gut. Giardia is a similar infection, with symptom including loose and foul-smelling diarrhoea, feeling bloated and nauseous, and stomach cramps. Giardia will recur without treatment, which is the same as for amoebic dysentery.

If suffering diarrhoea and/or vomiting try to rehydrate using oral rehydration salts (or, alternatively, one teaspoon each of salt and sugar in 500ml of water). If possible, avoid using imobilising drugs such as loperamide (Imodium) and atropine (Lomotil) as they prevent the body ridding itself of infection.

Skin and sun complaints

Prickly heat is a common complaint caused by excessive perspiration. Try to keep the skin dry by wearing loose-fitting cotton clothes. Sunburn is also a serious risk. Cover up and use a high-factor sunscreen, even if it is cloudy.

Heat exhaustion is indicated by shallow breathing, a rapid pulse, or pallour, and is often accompanied by leg cramps, headache or nausea. The body temperature remains normal. Lie down in a cool place and sip water mixed with rehydration salts or plain table salt.

Heatstroke is more serious, and more likely to occur when it is both hot and humid. Babies and the elderly are especially susceptible. The body temperature soars suddenly and the skin feels dry. The victim may feel confused, then pass out. Seek urgent medical help and take them quickly to a cool room, remove their clothes and cover them with a wet sheet or towels soaked in cold water.

INTERNET

Wi-fi is now widely available in India, including at virtually all hotels and guesthouses (often free, although sometimes chargeable in more expensive hotels). Internet cafes are becoming increasingly thin on the ground, although a few small ad hoc places can still be found both in major cities and tourist hangouts.

L

LGBTQ TRAVELLERS

Culturally, homosexuality remains a taboo subject for many Indians, especially in conservative rural areas. Homosexuality has been illegal in India since 1860. A 2009 ruling by the Delhi High Court decriminalised homosexuality, only for this decision to be reversed in 2013 – although an ongoing review by the Supreme Court may yet change the situation once more. For the time being, sexual relations between men are technically punishable with prison sentences, while cruising in public could come under public disorder laws – although actual prosecutions are extremely rare, and with a reasonable amount of discretion, gay and lesbian travellers to India are unlikely to encounter any problems, and hotels will think nothing of two men or women sharing a room. Be aware that although you'll often see men holding hands in India this doesn't mean they're gay, just good friends.

Useful online resources include www.travelgayasia.com and www.utopia-asia.com. Gay tours of India can be arranged through various operators including www.gaytripindia.com, www.indiapink.co.in and www.purpledrag.com/india.

M

MAPS

There are plenty of good maps of India. For Rajasthan, the best option is the *Reise Know How India North West* (Indien Nordwest) map, which has clear, accurate mapping and is printed on virtually indestructible waterproof and rip-proof paper. Finding good, detailed maps of individual cities is a lot trickier. Google Maps are far and away the best resource, although of course only available online, unless you've gone to the bother of downloading or screen-shotting the areas you need. The free maps handed out by hotels and tourists offices are generally unhelpful, and certainly not as good as the ones in this book.

You can buy maps at www.stanfords.co.uk, online home of the world-famous travel bookshop.

MEDIA

Newspapers and magazines

India has a long and strong journalist tradition (in English, Hindi and other languages) and its newspapers are amongst the best, and least censored, in Asia. Major English-language Indian newspapers include daily The Hindu (www.thehindu.com), The Hindustan Times (www.hindustantimes.com), the Indian Express (www.indianexpress.com) and the venerable The Times of India. (www.timesofindia.com). All are available in Rajasthan, at least the larger cities, although it's generally easier to read them online.

There's also a good selection of news magazines including Frontline (www.frontline.in), India Today (www.india-today.com), Outlook (www.outlookindia.com) and The Week (www.the-week.com).

Television and radio

Doordarshan is the government television company and broadcasts programmes in English, Hindi and regional languages.

Satellite television is available almost everywhere, with sets in most hotel rooms (and even in many guesthouses), although exactly how many channels you'll get is largely pot luck. The main local broadcaster is Star TV, whose network incorporates numerous foreign channels usually including the BBC World Service, CNN News, HBO, National Geographic, MTV and many others, as well as myriad local channels. NDTV is a local 24-hour news channel that provides good coverage of Indian news and politics. Other stations include Channel V (a local youth-orientated music channel) and Zee TV (Hindi and English).

All India Radio (AIR) broadcasts on various frequencies nationwide, while there are also various commercial stations broadcasting in English. The BBC World service and Voice of America can also be picked up on short-wave.

MONEY

The vast majority of travellers to India now carry plastic rather than travellers' cheques, and there are numerous ATMs in all larger cities accepted foreign Visa and MasterCards. However, away from the bigger towns, ATMs accepting foreign cards remain fairly thin on the ground, so it's a good idea to carry a reasonable amount of cash with you. If there's no ATM available, some banks will issue cash advances against credit cards over the counter. Credit cards are also accepted in many mid-range and upmarket hotels, more expensive restaurants and quite a few shops. If you do take travellers' cheques, stick to a well-known brand like Thomas Cook, American Express or Visa. Pounds sterling and US dollar banknotes are also easily changed either in banks or at official moneychangers; for other currencies you may have to locate a specialist bureau de change.

The Indian currency is the rupee, traditionally abbreviated to 'R' or 'Rs'. Coins come in denominations of Rs 1, 2, 5 and 10, notes in denominations of 5, 10, 20, 50, 100, 200, 500 and 2,000 (there are currently no 1,000 notes). Exchange rates as of late 2016 were £1 = Rs 85, US$1 = Rs 66 and €1 = Rs 75.

A service charge of 10 percent is often added to the bill in more upmarket restaurants and hotels. In addition, GST (government service charge; sometimes described as 'luxury tax') is levied in restaurants (either 12 or 18 percent) and in all but the cheapest guesthouses (at 18 or 28 percent). Always check whether quoted prices include all taxes (the so-called 'nett' price) or whether taxes are extra.

O

OPENING TIMES

Most shops open roughly 10am–6/7pm. More upmarket restaurants tend to open from around noon to 3pm and again from around 6pm to

10/11pm, although some stay open during the afternoon. Cafés (both cheap local dhabas and touristy cafes in places like Pushkar) generally open from around 8am until 10pm.

Most government offices are open 9.30am–6pm Monday–Friday, with a long lunch break.

Post offices are generally open 10am–4.30pm Monday–Friday, although central post offices in major cities also open at the weekend. Banks open roughly 10am–2pm weekdays and 10am–noon Saturday for most foreign banks and nationalised Indian banks (of which the State Bank is the largest). Some banks operate evening branches, while others remain open on Sunday and close on another day of the week, and some open 9am–1pm.

All banks, government office and post offices are closed on national holidays, although some shops and most restaurants stay open.

P

PHOTOGRAPHY

Most Rajasthanis love having their photos taken – although it's polite to ask before snapping away and to show them the results afterwards (assuming you're shooting in digital). Note, however, that some of the state's more conservative – and especially tribal – women will not appreciate having a camera pointed at them, however wonderfully photogenic they may look. You should also avoid taking photographs of military installations, bridges and dams, airports, border areas and Adivasi/restricted areas. Photography is prohibited in some temples, particularly in the inner shrine.

POST

International mail from India is slow and erratic, and you probably won't want to mail anything more valuable than a postcard while you're in the country. Stamps are generally only available from post offices.

If you need to mail anything of any value home while in India, you're best advised to use either a reputable international courier or EMS Speed Post rather than regular mail. You can send items by EMS from any major post office; rates to the UK are currently Rs 1390 for the first 0.25kg, and then Rs 110 for each additional 0.25kg (Rs 850/Rs 150 to the US). Take the items unwrapped to the post office before sending so that you can get customs clearance prior to packing.

Many shops offer to dispatch goods, although not all are reliable. By contrast, couriers are relatively expensive but offer peace of mind and quick delivery. DHL (www.logistics.dhl/in-en/home.html), Fedex (www.fedex.com/in) and UPS (www.ups.com/in) have offices in all the major cities.

PUBLIC HOLIDAYS

There are just three public holidays celebrated across India, Republic Day, Independence Day, and Gandhi Jayanti (celebrating the birth of Mahatma Gandhi). All other public holidays are set by the individual states – in Rajasthan these include a mix of Hindu, Jain, Sikh, Muslim and Christian festivals. Note that the exact dates of most holidays apart from the three national holidays change from year to year depending on the lunar calendar. Hindu festivals fall within the roughly the same period year on year (like the Western Easter), Islamic festivals change dates steadily year on year.

National holidays

26 January Republic Day

15 August Independence Day

2 October Gandhi Jayanti

Rajasthan holidays

Early January Guru Gobind Singh Jayanti

Late February/early March Maha Shivaratri

March Holi

14 April Dr Ambedkar Jayanti

April Rama Navami

April Mahavir Jayanthi

August Raksha Bandhan

August Janmashtami/Sri Krishna Jayanti

Late September/early October Dussehra

October Diwali

Early November Guru Nanak Jayanti

Variable dates Id ul Fitr

Variable dates Muharram

Variable dates Milad un Nabi

PUBLIC TRANSPORT

By air

India has an excellent network of domestic air, with connections between pretty much every major city in the country. The main carriers are
Air India (www.airindia.in), Jet Airways (www.jetairways.com), SpiceJet
(www.spicejet.com), IndiGo (www.goindigo.in) and GoAir (www.goair.in).
The websites www.skyscanner.com and www.expedia.co.in are probably the most useful resources for working out what's available and for
booking tickets.

There are four passenger airports in Rajasthan: **Jaipur International
Airport** (tel: 0141 255 0623, www.jaipurairport.com), **Jodhpur Airport**
(tel: 0291 251 2934), **Udaipur's Maharana Pratap Airport** (tel: 0294 265
5950, www.udaipurairport.com), and the recently opened Jaisalmer
Airport (tel: 02992 250 048). All four have direct connections with both
Delhi and Mumbai. Within Rajasthan there are useful direct flights between Jaipur and Udaipur and Jaipur and Jaisalmer, although to fly
between other cities within the state you'll need to transit via Delhi or
Jaipur.

By rail

Rail travel is safe, reasonably comfortable and by far the most enjoyable way to get around Rajasthan, with regular services between all the
major cities, and many smaller towns as well. The system is somewhat

complicated, but it's well worth mastering the basics. For further information see the excellent www.seat61.com/India.htm, while full timetables are available at Indian Railways' official websites, www.indianrail.gov.in and www.irctc.co.in.

Various different types of train are available. Indian Railways' premier services are the Shatabdi or Rajdhani expresses: high-speed, top-quality trains travelling either by day (Shatabdi) or overnight (Rajdhani), with meals are included in the fare. As well as Shatabdi and Rajdhani services, there are also numerous long-distance services designated as 'Express', 'Intercity' or 'Superfast'. 'Mail' services are slower, and generally run overnight. 'Passenger' services are slow local trains.

There are no less than eight different classes of travel available across all services (although most trains have only three or four classes, varying according to the type of service, whether local, long-distance, express and so on). Most expensive sleeper classes include **AC first class** ('1A'), with comfortable, lockable cabins of two or four berths each; and **AC two-tier** ('2A') and **three-tier** ('3A'), with partitioned compartments of six and nine curtained berths respectively. Daytime Shatabdi services also have **AC Executive chair class ('EC') and AC chair class ('CC')**, with spacious seating in AC carriages.

Cheaper classes include **Sleeper class** ('SL'), comprising non-AC six berths compartments – perfectly acceptable if you're prepared to do without AC, although hot in summer. **Second class** ('2S', or 'Second sitting') is either reserved or unreserved but with no berths. Seats are sometimes padded, although some carriages in unreserved have unpadded wooden seats. This class is usually acceptable for short daytime journeys of an hour or two, but is otherwise best avoided, and unreserved carriages can often get crowded.

Buying tickets

Reservations are required for all tickets apart from second class unreserved – be aware that tickets on popular services often sell out weeks in advance, so the earlier you can book the better. To reserve in person, go to the booking office and fill out a Reservation Requisition Form with your passport number, the train number and name, the required class and (for overnight journeys) preferred berth. If you want to avoid the hassle of visiting the station, be aware that many hotels, guesthouses and local travel agents can book railway tickets for you for a small fee.

All major stations now have efficient computerised booking counters from where you can book any ticket for any route. You can also buy tickets online at various sites including, most easily, at www.12go.asia, and also (with more difficulty) at www.irctc.co.in and www.cleartrip.com. All accept payment by foreign Visa and MasterCards, meaning that you can book tickets in advance from abroad. Reservations may be made up to 120 days in advance on some trains, although sometimes it's just 60, 30 or even 15 days. In the larger cities (including Jaipur), stations have tourist sections with English-speaking staff to reduce the queues for foreigners.

Places on some trains tend to sell out quickly (check availability at www.indianrail.gov.in or www.irctc.co.in). If you can't get a ticket there are three options. A few seats are reserved under the 'Foreign Tourist Quota' (FTC), although these can only be bought in person at a station and must be paid for in US dollars, pounds sterling or rupees backed by an exchange certificate (although an ATM receipt will probably do).

If all the FTC seats have gone, there are also a number of seats on certain trains (marked with a 'T' in timetables) reserved under the Taktal scheme. These tickets cost a bit more and are released just one day in advance, but can also be booked online.

At the station and on board

Indian trains can be huge, and finding your seat/berth can be half the fun. Lists of passengers and the compartment and seat/berth numbers allotted to them are displayed on platforms and on each carriage an hour before departure. If your train hasn't arrived, ask the station superintendent roughly where on the platform your carriage will arrive.

Cloakrooms are available at most stations where you can leave your luggage, but bags must be locked, and don't lose the reclaim ticket. Check opening times of the cloakroom for collection.

On board, food can usually be ordered through the coach attendant, while roving snack-sellers and coffee/tea vendors often roam the comparments in search of custom. Bedding is provided on overnight first-class services. If travelling second-class sleeper it's a good idea to take a sheet or blanket. Carriages on all trains have either Western and Indian-style toilets.

Special trains

There are two 'royal trains' through Rajasthan (and parts of other states), offering tours in luxurious live-aboard carriages. The most famous is the world-renowned The Palace on Wheels (www.palaceonwheels.co.uk), comprising 23 superb Raj-era style carriages, with weekly departures from Delhi between September and April. The seven-night tours stop at Jaipur, Bharatpur, Chittaurgarh, Udaipur, Ranthambore, Jaisalmer, Jodhpur, Bharatpur and Agra. Prices are $4,975 per week in a double cabin (reduced to $3830 in September and April).

Equally luxurious, although less characterful, the Maharaja's Express (www.the-maharajas.com) offers tours of three and seven nights, focusing mainly on Rajasthan and Agra. Tours cost from $3,850 per person for the three-night tours, and $5,980 for seven-night trips.

Buses

Despite Rajasthan's extensive railway network, there may be times when buses are quicker or more convenient, albeit less comfortable. Getting around Shekhawati, for example, is tricky by train but easy by bus. Equally, although there are trains to Jaisalmer, you may find timings for the daytime bus more convenient, while Bikaner is also often easier to reach by road than rail. As well as buses within the state there are also numerous express buses between Delhi and Jaipur (and other destinations in Rajsthan), although for this journey the train is significantly faster and more comfortable.

Types of bus vary widely. At the top end of the scale the major inter-city routes are served by 'luxury' or 'deluxe' air-conditioned express services. At the bottom end of the scale, rural buses are often noisy rustbuckets which can sometimes get packed to the gills. Most services fall somewhere between the two. Government buses are operated by the RSRTC (Rajasthan State Road Transport Corporation; www.transport.rajasthan.gov.in/rsrtc) while private buses are run by myriad private companies. Seats can be reserved on many services, even local ones, at the relevant bus station. Alternatively, your guesthouse or hotel should be able to arrange this for you for a small fee and save you some precious time.

Rickshaws and taxis

Within towns and cities, the most convenient and often the quickest way of getting around is by rickshaw – a quintessentially Indian experience as you weave and duck through the traffick. Rickshaws come in two types: motorised three-wheelers known as an 'auto-rickshaws' or just 'autos', and human-powered cycle rickshaws – the latter are becoming increasingly rare in the cities and are now used mainly in smaller towns and rural areas. They can also be excruciatingly slow, and although okay for short hops are best avoided for longer journeys.

Fares in all rickshaws are agreed by bargaining, and should always be negotiated in advance with the driver – bargain hard. Some autos are equipped with meters, although even when fitted drivers are usually extremely reluctant to use them, generally claiming that they're 'broken' – the idea being that they can charge you more by bartering a fare. It's a good idea to ask at your hotel how much you should pay for a ride before heading out, so you have some idea of what the going rate is, although expect to pay more than the local price.

As well as hiring autos for single journeys, it's also common to book one for short tours. Again, agree a fare in advance and be absolutely clear where you do and do not want to go – rickshaws drivers often earn commission by taking tourists to shops and it's not uncommon for drivers to attempt to drag visitors into local souvenir emporiums rather than sticking to the agreed itinerary.

There are also a number of modern radio taxi firms in the major cities, which can be booked for short trips or longer tours. Fares are metered and come in at around Rs.20/km (a bit more at night). This compares very favourably with what you might pay in an autorickshaw, while taxis are obviously much more comfortable – although not so good at finding a way through heavy traffic. Leading operators include **Metro Cabs in Jaipur** (tel: 0141 333 4000, www.metrocabs.in), Jodhpur Cabs in Jodhpur (tel: 0766 545 4999, www.jodhpurcabs.com), and Rajasthan Cabs in **Udaipur** (tel: 093 5132 4541, www.rajasthancabs.co.in). You can also book cabs using mobile apps including Uber and Ola in the major cities.

R

RELIGION

The government of India is secular, and no faith is recognized as an official national religion. The majority of Rajasthanis (over 85 percent) are Hindu, and there are also large numbers of Jains and – in certain parts of the state – Muslims. There are also a fair number of Sikhs (mainly in the cities) and a small number of Christians. All religions are free to practice their faiths, and communal religious tensions are rare – unlike some other parts of India, and despite the best efforts of the ruling BJP. There are churches (mainly Catholic) in all the larger cities.

S

SMOKING

Around 120 million people smoke in India (12 percent of all the world's smokers), while increasing prosperity has led to a sharp increase in the number of people using cigarettes – up 36 percent between 1998 and 2015. It has also become increasingly fashionable (even the male heroes in Bollywood films now light up, whereas in the past smoking was the exclusive preserve of cinematic villains). Smoking is banned in all the usual places: offices, airports (except in designated smoking rooms), at railway and bus stations, on buses and trains, and in restaurants (with the possible exception of some outdoor restaurants or designated smoking areas) and some hotels.

T

TELEPHONES

India's telephone system is slowly improving but still far from perfect and many Indians use mobile phones rather than landlines. Privately run telephone services with international direct-dialling facilities are widespread, advertising themselves with the acronyms STD/ISD (standard trunk dialling/international subscriber dialling). Note that calling from hotels can be extremely expensive, with surcharges of up to 300 percent, so check rates first.

If you're going to making a lot of calls while you're in India, it's well worth buying a local SIM card, costing just a few dollars and available from any of the myriad phone shops which can be found in all towns (you'll need to show your passport). Charges for both domestic and international calls using an Indian SIM card will be far lower than what you'll pay using your own phone from home. You can put the Indian SIM in your own phone if it's unlocked; if not, you can always pick up a cheap handset for as little as £10/$13.

If you want to use your own mobile and SIM while in India, you'll need to check if you need to have it unblocked in order to work abroad and what roaming charges will apply. European (GSM) mobiles generally work fine in India, although North American CDMA handsets do not.

To call abroad from India, dial the international access code (00), the code for the country you want (44 for the UK, 1 for the US or Canada), the appropriate area code (without any initial zeros), and the number you want. To call India from abroad, dial the international access code (00, or 001 from North America), followed by 91 for India, the local code minus the initial zero, then the number.

TIME ZONES

India is 5.5 hours ahead of Greenwich Mean Time; 10 hours 30mins ahead of Eastern Standard Time (east coast US and Canada), 13 hours 30min ahead of Pacific Standard Time (west coast US and Canada), and 4 hours 30min behind eastern Australian.

TIPPING

IWestern and Indian styles of tipping are somewhat different. The Western idea of tipping waiters and hotel staff isn't really widespread but is, of course, always be appreciated if you've received good service. Ten percent of the bill in a restaurant is sufficient. Note also that many more upmarket hotels and restaurants add a 10 percent 'service charge' to the bill, which should cover tips – although, equally, this may not find its way to the staff involved, so you might want to add something extra on top. Tipping rickshaw and taxi drivers isn't generally expected unless they've gone significantly out of their way to help you.

Indian-style tipping takes the form of baksheesh. This applies in any situation where someone offers you assistance of any kind: carrying your bags, showing you around a temple, leading you to your hotel, getting you a seat on a train, and so on. It's customary in such circumstances to offer some sort of token of your appreciation – there's no hard and fast rule about how much and you'll have to use your own judgement depending on what sort of help you've received.

TOILETS

There are very few public toilets in India, and where they exist they're generally filthy. If you get caught short head for the nearest hotel or, failing that, a good-looking restaurant or cafe, where available. If you're out in the countryside you'll just have to find a likely looking tree or bush. Western-style toilets are increasingly becoming the norm across the country, although you'll still encounter quite a few traditional 'squat' toilets.

TOURIST INFORMATION

The main Indian Ministry of Tourism website is www.incredibleindia. org, while the Rajasthan government has its own tourism site at www. tourism.rajasthan.gov.in. There are government-run RTDC (Rajasthan Tourism Development Corporation) tourist offices in Jaipur, Jodhpur, Bikaner, Jaisalmer, Udaipur, Pushkar, Ranthambore, Bharatpur and elsewhere. How useful they are depends very much on the knowledge and helpfulness of whoever happens to be behind the desk at the time – some can be very helpful and clued-up, others can be a waste of time. All these offices can also arrange tours and transport. In general, however, you'll often get equally good – and often considerably better – tourist information either from staff at your guesthouse/hotel or from a local tour operator/travel agent (although travel agent information might of course not be entirely impartial). .

Indian tourist offices abroad

Australia: Shop 35, Level 1, Stockland Piccadilly, 133 Castlereagh Street, Sydney NSW, tel: 02-9267 2466.

Canada: 60 Bloor Street West, Suite 1003, Toronto, Ontario M4 N3 N6, tel: 416-962 3787–8.

South Africa: Hyde Park Lane Manor, Lancaster Gate, Hyde Park 2196, Cnr of Jan Smuts Avenue & William Nicole Drive, Johannesburg 2000, tel: 011-325 0880.

UK 26–28 Hammersmith Grove, London W6 7BA, tel: 020-7437 3677.

US 1270 Avenue of the Americas, Suite 303, New York 10020, tel: 212-

586 4901–3; 3550 Wilshire Boulevard, Suite 204, Los Angeles, California 90010 2485, tel: 0213-380 8855.

Local tourist offices

Delhi

India Tourism, 88 Janpath, New Delhi, tel: 011-2332 0005, 2332 0008.

Jaipur

RTDC, Hotel Swagatam, near the railway station, tel: 0141-220 2586
India Tourism, Hotel Khasa Kothi, tel: 0141-236 0112

V

VISAS AND PASSPORTS

All travellers except citizens of Nepal and Bhutan require a visa to enter India. Fees and the types of visa available vary according to where you're from, although costs can be high (from £110 for UK citizens, for example). Citizens of most countries can apply for a visa online, with a bewildering number of websites offering this service, although it's best to stick to the government-run www.indianvisaonline.gov.in – if in doubt, check with your local Indian embassy or consulate. Most tourist visas are issued for a maximum of 60 days and cannot be extended. Both single and multiple-entry visas available, although they generally cost the same.

RECOMMENDED HOTELS

Most of Rajasthan's more expensive accommodation can be found either in so-called 'heritage hotels' set in converted palaces, forts or havelis, or in modern replicas of traditional buildings. There are literally hundreds of such places across the state, from traditional city-centre palaces and havelis (mansions) to remote forts, in every conceivable shape and size. Some of the cheaper places are stronger on atmosphere than on creature comforts and modern facilities, although the very best places, like the famous Umaid Bhawan Palace in Jodhpur or the Rambagh Palace in Jaipur, offer the quintessence of Indian style and luxury at suitably stratospheric prices.

$$$$$	Rs 20,000 and above
$$$$	Rs 10,000–20,000
$$$	Rs 4,000–10,000
$$	Rs 1,500–4,000
$	up to Rs 1,500

AJMER

Badnor House $$ *Civil Lines, tel: 0145 262 7579*, www.badnorhouse.com. Peaceful and friendly guesthouse with comfortable and spacious rooms in a pretty little modern house. Horse safaris and local sightseeing trips can be arranged.

BHARATPUR

Iora Guest House $ *Gauri Shankar Colony, tel: 098 2804 1294*, www.iora guesthouse.com. Run by a local naturalist and photographer, this is one of Bharatpur's stand-out budget options, with neat and inexpensive rooms and a nice little restaurant.

Laxmi Vilas Palace $$$ *Kakaji ki Kothi, tel: 05644 231 199*, www.laxmivilas.com. Bharatpur's most memorable place to stay, set in a converted palace on the outskirts of town. Rooms and public areas are full of traditional character, while facilities include a pretty restaurant and a large pool.

BIKANER

Tanisha Heritage Haveli $ *Asasniyon ka Chowk, tel: 075 6802 5662.* Budget lodgings in a wonderful old haveli at the heart of the old city, with colourfully decorated rooms, excellent home cooking and a very friendly welcome.

Vinayak Guest House $ *Mehron ka Bas, tel: 094 1443 0948.* Simple, inexpensive lodgings in a friendly and centrally located family guesthouse. They can also arrange excellent camel safaris and wildlife trips (www.vinayakdesertsafari.com).

BUNDI

Dev Niwas $$ *Opposite Purani Kotwali, tel: 082 3334 5394,* www.jagat-collection.com. Small heritage hotel in an atmospheric 300-year-old haveli. The attractive rooms and beautifully decorated public areas belie the relatively modest rooms rates, and there are sweeping views from the neat rooftop restaurant.

Hotel Bundi Haveli $ *107 Balchand Parra, tel: 074 7244 6716,* www.hotelbundihaveli.com. Imposing traditional haveli on the edge of the old town that has been given a chic contemporary makeover. The cool white rooms have panoramic views from traditional jharokha window seats, and there's good food in the stylish little restaurant. Good value.

CHITTAURGARH

Fort Begu $$$$ *Begu village, 65km east of Chittaurgarh, tel: 094 6092 0444,* www.fortbegu.com. Set in a dramatic 15th-century fort out in the depths of the countryside between Chittaurgarh and Kota, this stunning heritage hotel offers an authentic taste of the region's living history and culture, with picture-perfect rooms individually decorated in traditional Rajasthani style.

JAIPUR

Pearl Palace Heritage $$ *54 Gopal Bari, Lane 2, Ajmer Road, tel: 0141 237 5242,* www.pearlpalaceheritage.com. This stunningly decorated little hotel is without doubt Jaipur's best bargain, stunningly decorated in an eye-boggling array of traditional crafts, paintings and fabrics from across Rajasthan and further afield. Given the quality, prices are unbelievably low.

Pearl Palace Hotel $$ *51 Hathroi Fort , Hari Kishan Somani Marg, Ajmer Road, tel: 0141 237 3700,* www.hotelpearlpalace.com. One of the best budget hotels not just in Jaipur but in the whole of India, with very comfortable rooms, an outstanding little rooftop restaurant, plus very friendly and super-efficient staff happy to arrange just about anything you might need.

Rambagh Palace Hotel $$$$$ *Bhawani Singh Road, tel: 0141 238 5700,* www.tajhotels.com. One of the country's most memorable heritage hotels, set in the 19th-century palace which was once home to the maharaja of Jaipur. The spectacular building and gorgeous gardens are the main attraction, backed up with opulently decorated rooms and top-notch dining and drinking facilities.

Samode Haveli $$$$$ *Gangapole, tel: 0141 263 2407,* www.samode.com. Hidden away on the edge of the Pink City, this 150-year-old converted haveli doesn't boast the lavish comforts and extensive facilities of other top city hotels but compensates with its brilliantly central location, wonderful old-fashioned Rajasthani interiors and memorably time-warped atmosphere.

Shahpura House $$$$ *D-257, Devi Marg, Bani Park, tel: 0141 408 9100,* www.shahpura.com. One of the city's most lavishly decorated mid-range hotels, full of colourful murals and traditional decorative touches. Rooms are comfortably furnished and individually designed, and there's also a nice restaurant.

Sunder Palace Guest House $ *Sanjay Marg, Hathroi Fort, Ajmer Road,* *tel: 0141 236 0178,* www.sunderpalace.com. Rivalling the nearby Pearl Palace for the title of Jaipur's best budget option, this outstanding guesthouse boasts very comfortable and attractively appointed rooms, super-sharp service and quality food in the garden café and rooftop restaurant.

Taj Jai Mahal Palace Hotel $$$$$ *Jacob Road, Civil Lines, tel: 0141* *222, 3636,* www.tajhotels.com. Classy but relatively affordable Taj hotel set in a huge Indo-Saracenic palace of 1745 conveniently located for the city centre. Rooms are attractively decorated with traditional fabrics and artworks, and amenities include lovely gardens plus pool.

JAISALMER

The Gulaal $$$ *Opposite Nagarpalika, tel: 02992 251 450,* www.thegulaal.com. This beautifully designed 'luxury boutique haveli' offers plenty of traditional ambience, with attractive sandstone buildings arranged around a pair of intimate courtyards. There's also a garden pool, Ayurvedic spa and lovely fort views.

Killa Bhawan $$$ *Jaisalmer Fort, 445 Kotri Para, tel: 02992 251 204,* www.killabhawan.com. Romantic boutique hotel occupying two townhouses within the fort, with traditional decor and a beautiful roof terrace covered in bolsters and cushions offering superb sunset views.

Shahi Palace $$ *Shiv Rd, tel: 02992 255 920,* www.shahipalacehotel.com. Stylish and affordable little boutique guesthouse just south of town. Rooms are cool and attractively furnished with polished sandstone and colourful fabrics, and there are great fort views from the rooftop terrace.

Suraj $$ *Jaisalmer Fort, by the Jain Temples. tel: 096 0227 2345,* www.hotelsurajhaveli.com. Simple but hugely atmospheric guesthouse, set in a beautiful old converted haveli deep inside the fort, with wonderful views of the nearby Jain temples.

Suryagarh $$$$ *Sam Road, around 15km from Jaisalmer, tel: 02992 269 269,* www.suryagarh.com. Set in an impressive fort-style complex out in the desert, Suryagarh's designs blend traditional Rajasthan motifs with chic contemporary styling, while amenities include a lovely indoor pool and rooftop dining with stunning desert views.

JODHPUR

Govind Hotel $ *Station Road, tel: 0291 262 2758,* www.govindhotel.com. Stand-out budget option, with simple but clean and very comfortable rooms plus friendly and very professional service. The rooftop restaurant is also a great place to try traditional Rajasthani specialities which you'll rarely find on menus elsewhere.

Haveli Inn Pal $$$ *Near Gulab Sagar Lake, tel: 094 1414 5479,* www.haveliinnpal.com. One of the best places to stay inside the old city itself, this imposing old haveli has spacious, comfortably equipped rooms and a superb rooftop restaurant with peerless fort views.

Ratan Villas $$$ *Loco Shed Road, tel: 0291 261 4418,* www.ratanvilas.com. Peaceful retreat set in a 1920s mansion with spacious colonial-style rooms and an exquisite candlelit courtyard restaurant. There's also a nice pool; local village tours can be arranged too.

Singhvi's Haveli $ *Ramdeo Ji ka Chowk, Navchokiya, tel: 0291 262 4293,* www.singhvihaveli.com. Jodphur at its most historic, occupying a beautiful 500-year-old haveli on the quieter western side of the old city, with inexpensive, attractively furnished rooms, and superb fort views.

Umaid Bhawan Palace $$$$$ *Circuit House Road, tel: 0291 251 0101,* www.tajhotels.com. Set in India's most spectacular Art Deco palace, the Umaid Bhawan was rated the world's best hotel by TripAdvisor in 2016 and is without doubt one of India's most memorable (and expensive) places to stay. The vast rooms are luxuriously equipped, while the huge gardens, stunning restaurants, superb pool and spa, plus service fit for a maharaja, all add to the allure.

MOUNT ABU

Connaught House $$$ *Rajendra Marg, tel: 02974 238 560*, www.welcom
heritagehotels.in. Near Nakki Lake in the centre of town, the former
summer residence of the Chief Minister of Marwar boasts heaps of pe-
riod character, with ten beautifully appointed period rooms set in peace-
ful gardens.

PUSHKAR

Inn Seventh Heaven $$ *Next to the Mali ka Mandir, tel: 0145 297 1905*,
www.inn-seventh-heaven.com. This easy-to-miss boutique retreat
looks like a typical old-fashioned haveli from the outside but has plenty
of alluring contemporary style inside, with an airy courtyard surrounded
by vine-covered balconies and a range of attractively furnished but surprisingly inexpensive rooms.

Kanhaia Haveli $ *Near Mali Mandir, Chotti Basti, tel: 094 1436 4046.* www.
pushkarhotelkanhaia.com. Four-star style at one-star prices is the
hallmark of this attractive little boutique hotel, with neat and colourful
rooms set around a gorgeous plant-filled courtyard.

RANTHAMBORE

Sher Bagh $$$$$ *Sherpur, Khiljipur, tel: 011 4617 2700*, www.sujanluxury.
com/sher-bagh. Originally designed for the Maharaja of Jaipur's hunting expeditions, this intimate forest camp offers a deluxe back-to-na-
ture experience in opulent tents nestled up close to the fringes of the
national park.

SAMODE

Samode Palace $$$$$ *Samode, tel: 0141 263 2370*, www.samode.com.
Dominating the small village of Samode near Jaipur, this vast palace is
home to one of Rajasthan's most famous heritage hotels, with magnificent Indo-Saracenic interiors including a spectacular shish mahal (hall
of mirrors).

SHEKHAWATI

Apani Dhani $$ *Jhunjhunu Road, Nawalgarh, tel: 01594 222 239*, www.apanidhani.com. Long-running and deservedly popular 'eco-farm' on the edge of Nawalgarh. Accommodation is in cosy miniature bungalows designed in traditional Rajasthani style and there's also good vegetarian food and rewarding local tours and activities on offer.

Mandawa Haveli $$ *Near Sonthaliya Gate, Mandawa, tel: 01592 223 088*, www.hotelmandawahaveli.com. Wonderfully atmospheric – and refreshingly inexpensive – haveli with lavish rooms, some still covered in their original murals.

Roop Niwas Kothi $$$ *Nawalgarh, tel: 01594 222 008*, www.roopniwaskothi.com. Appealing upper mid-range hotel in a large 1920s mansion with spacious and comfortable rooms that have plenty of enjoyable colonial character. There are lovely gardens, plus a good restaurant and pool too.

Vivaana $$$ *Mandawa, tel: 098 1127 6231*, www.vivaana.com. Excellent hotel in a stunning traditional haveli. The beautifully decorated interiors and immaculate rooms are amongst the best in town, while facilities include a pool and Ayurvedic spa. Horse and camel safaris can also be arranged.

UDAIPUR

Amet Haveli $$$ *Nr Chandpole, tel: 0294 243 1085*, www.amethaveliudaipur.com. Lovely lakeside haveli with beautifully decorated rooms including spacious suites right over the water. The attached Ambrai garden restaurant is also excellent.

Bhanwar Vilas Guest House $ *Gangaur Ghat, tel: 294 241 1576*, www.bhanwarvilasudaipur.com. Homely little 'heritage guesthouse' run by a leading local tourist guide offering cosy rooms decorated with colourful rugs and fabrics, plus good traditional Indian vegetarian cooking.

Jaiwana Haveli $$$ *Lalghat, tel: 0294 241 1103*, www.jaiwanahaveli.com. Close to Lake Pichola, this well-run hotel has modern rooms (some with lake views) in a fine old traditional building, plus good rooftop restaurant.

Panorama Guest House $ *Hanuman Ghat, tel: 0294 243 1027*, www. panoramaguesthouse.in. Excellent budget guesthouse in a tall skinny house next to the lake. Rooms are neat and well-maintained, and there's also a nice little rooftop café and very helpful staff.

RAAS Devigarh $$$$$ *Delwara, tel: 0291 263 6455*, www.raasdevigarh. com. Located 16 miles (26km) from Udaipur, this impressive fort is now one of Rajasthan's finest hotels. The fort's towering exterior retains its traditional craggy splendour, while interiors have been given a very chic modern makeover, with every conceivable luxury, including a wonderful pool and spa.

Taj Lake Palace Hotel $$$$$ *Pichola Lake, tel: 0294 242 8800*, www.taj hotels.com. One of the world's most romantic hotels, set in a gleaming white palace that seems to float magically on the waters of Lake Pichola. Rooms and suites are beautifully furnished, and the view over the lake from the restaurant is one of India's great sights.

DICTIONARY

A

a few सिर्फ़ कुछ *sirf kuch*

a little थोड़ा *thodaa*

a lot बहुत *bahut*

a.m. पूर्वाह्न *purvahaan*

abbey मठ *muth*

about (approximately) लगभग *lugbhug*

abroad विदेश में *videsh mein*

accept, to स्वीकार करना *sweekaar karnaa*

access only केवल प्रवेश *kewal pravesh*

accident (road) दुर्घटना *durghatnaa*

accompany, to साथ देना *aath dena*

acne मुँहासा *muhaansaa*

acrylic ऐक्रिलिक *acrylic*

actor/actress अभिनेता/अभिनेत्री *abhineta/abhinetree*

adapter एडेप्टर *adapter*

address पता *pata*

adjoining room आसन्न कमरा *aasun kumra*

admission charge प्रवेश शुल्क *pravesh shulk*

adult (n) बड़े *bade*

after (time) बाद में *baad mein*

after-shave आफ्टर शेव *after-shave*

after-sun lotion आफ्टर-सन लोशन

after-sun lotion

afternoon, in the दोपहर में *dopeher mein*

aged: to be ~ उम्रदराज: उम्रदराज होना *umerd-araaz : umerdaraaz hona*

ago पहले *pehle*

agree: I don't agree सहमत होना: मैं सहमत नहीं *sehmat hona: main sehmat nahin*

air: ~ conditioning हवा: वातानुकूलित हवा: *vatanakulit;* **~ mattress** हवा वाली गद्दी *hava waali gaddi;* **~ pump** हवा भरने वाला *hava bharne waala;* **~ sickness bag** बीमारी वाली थैली *bimaari waali theli;* **~ mail** हवाई मेल *hawaai mail*

airport एयरपोर्ट *airport*

aisle seat गलियारे के पास वाली सीट *galiyaari ke paas waali seat*

alarm clock अलार्म घड़ी *alarm ghadi*

alcoholic (drink) ड्रिंक *drink*

all सब *sub*

allergic, to be एलर्जी होना *allergy hona*

allergy एलर्जी *allergy*

allowance भत्ता *bhatta*

almost लगभग *lugbhug*

alone अकेला *akelaa*

already पहले से *pehle se*

also भी *bhi*

alter, to परिवर्तित करना *parvartit kurnaa*

alumin(i)um foil एल्युमिनियम फॉयल *aluminium foil*

always हमेशा *hameshaa*

a.m. पूर्वाह्न *purvahaan*

am: I am हूँ: मैं हूँ *hoon: main hoon*

amazing अद्भुत *adbhut*

ambassador राजदूत *raajdoot*

ambulance एंबुलेंस *ambulance*

American अमेरिकन *american*

amount राशि *raashi*

anaesthetic बेहोशी *behoshi*

and और *aur*

animal जानवर *jaanwar*

anorak टोपीदार बरसाती कोट *topidaar barsaati coat*

another अन्य *anya*

antacid एंटासिड *antacid*

antibiotics एंटिबायोटिक *antibiotic*

antifreeze एंटीफ्रीज *antifreeze*

antique प्राचीन *pracheen~* **store** प्रा. चीन वस्तुओं की दुकान

pracheen vustuaon kee dukaan

antiseptic एंटिसेप्टिक *antiseptic~* **cream** एंटीसेप्टिक क्रीम *antiseptic cream*

any कोई *koi*

anyone: ~ else कोई भी: कोई और *koi bhi; koi aur*

does anyone speak English? क्या कोई अंग्रेज़ी बोलता है? *kya koi angrezee boltaa hai?*

apartment अपार्टमेंट *apartment*

apologize: I apologize माफ़ी: मैं माफ़ी चाहता हूँ *maafi: main maafi chattaa hoon*

appendicitis अपेंडिसाइ. टिस *appendicitis*

appendix अपेंडिक्स *appendix*

appetite भूख *appetite*

appointment (to make an …) अपॉयन्टमेंट (अपॉयन्टमेंट लेना) *appointment (appoint-ment lena)*

approximately लगभग *lugbhug*

April अप्रैल *april*

architect आर्किटेक्ट *architect*

are there…? क्या … हैं? *kya …hai?*

arm बाँह *baanh*
around लगभग *lugbhug*
arrive, to पहुंचना *pahoonchnaa*
art gallery आर्ट गैलरी *art gallery*
arthritis, to have गठिया होना *gathiyaa hona*
artificial sweetener कृत्रिम मीठा बनाने वाला *kritrim meetha banane waala*
artist कलाकार *kalakaar*
ashtray ऐश ट्रे *ash tray*
ask: I asked for पूछा: मैंने ... के लिए पूछा *poocha: maine...ke liye poocha*
aspirin एस्पिरन *asprin*
asthma, to have दमा होना *dama hona*
at पर *pur*
athletics एथलेटिक्स *athletics*
ATM/cash machine ए टी एम *ATM machine* मशीन *machine*
attack हमला *humlaa*
attractive आकर्षक *akurshuk*
August अगस्त *agast*
aunt चाची *chachee*
Australia आस्ट्रेलिया *australia*
Australian आस्ट्रेलियन *australian*
authentic: is it authentic? वास्तविक: क्या यह वास्तविक है? *vastavik: kya yeh vastavik hai*
authenticity वास्. विकता *vastaviktaa*

automatic ~car स्वचालित *swachalit*~**camera** स्वचालित कैमरा *swachalit camera*
automobile ऑटोमा. *baaijl automobile*
autumn शरद *sharad*
avalanche एवालांश *avalanche*
away (from) दूर (से) *door (se)*
awful बेकार *bekaar*

B
baby बच्चा *baccha*; ~**food** बेबी फूड *baby food*; ~**wipes** बेबी वाईप्स *baby wipes*; ~-**sitter** बेबी-सिटर *baby sitter*
back पीछे *peeche* ~**ache** पीठ का दर्द *peeth kaa dard*
backpacking बैक पैकिंग *back packing*
bad बुरा *bura*
bag बैग *bag*
baggage सामान *samaan*
bakery बेकरी *bakery*
balcony बालकनी *balkani*
ball गेंद *gend*
band बैंड *baind*
bandage बैंडेज *bandage*
bank बैंक *bank*
bar बार *bar*
barber नाई *nai*
basement तहखाना *tehkhaana*
basket बास्केट *basket*
basketball बास्केटबॉल *basketball*
bath स्नान *snaan*; ~ **towel** तौलिया *tauliyaa*

bathroom (toilet) शौचालय *shauchalaya* [with bath] स्नान के साथ *snaan ke saath*
battery बैटरी *battery*
battle site युद्ध स्थल *yudh sthal*
be, to होना *hona*
beach समुद्र-तट *sanudra-tut*
beard दाढी *daadhi*
beautiful खूबसूरत *khubsoorat*
because (of) कारण *kaaran*
bed बिस्तर *bistar*~ **and breakfast** बिस्तर और नाश्ता *bistar aur breakfast*
bedding बिस्तर *bistar*
bedroom शयनकक्ष *shyankaksh*
beer बीयर *beer*
before से पहले *se pehle*
begin, to आरंभ करना *aarambh kurnaa*
beige मटमैला *mutmela*
belong: this belongs to me किसी का होना: यह मेरा है *kisi ka hona:yeh mera hai*
belt बेल्ट *belt*
best सबसे अच्छा *sabse acha*
better ज्यादा अच्छा *jyadaa acha*
between बीच में *beech mein*~ **jobs** नौकरी के बीच में *naukri ke beech mein*
bib बिप *peena*
bicycle साइकिल *cycle*; ~ **hire** किराए का साइकिल *kiraaye ka cycle*

bidet बिडे *bide*
big बड़ा *bada*
bigger ज्यादा बड़ा *jyadaa bada*
bikini बिकिनी *bikini*
bill बिल *bill*
binoculars दूरबीन *doorbeen*
bird पक्षी *pakshi*
birthday जन्मदिन *janamdin*
biscuits बिस्कुट *biscuit*
bite (insect) काटना *kaatnaa*
bitten: I've been bitten by a dog काट लिया: मुझे कुत्ते ने काट लिया ह *kaat liya: mujhe kutte ne kaat liya hai*
bitter कड़वा *kadwaa*
bizarre विचित्र *vitchitra*
black काली *kaali*; ~ **and white** श्वेत और श्याम *shwet aur shyam*
bladder मूत्राशय *mutrashay*
blanket कंबल *kambal*
bleach ब्लीच *bleach*
bleeding खून बहना *khoon behnaa*
blinds परदा *pardaa*
blister फोड़ा *phodaa*
blocked, to be बाधित, होना *baadhit hona*
blood रक्त *rukt*; ~ **group** ब्लड ग्रुप *blood group*; ~ **pressure (high)** रक्तचाप (उच्च) *ruktchaap (uchh)*
blouse ब्लाउज़ *blouse*
blue नीला *neela*
board, on बोर्ड पर *board pur*
boat नौका *nauka*; ~ **trip** नौका यात्रा *nauka yatra*

boil उबलना *ubulnaa*

boiled उबला *ublaa*

boiler उबालने के लिए बर्तन *ubulne ke liye bartan*

bone हड्डी *huddi*

book पुस्तक *pustak*; **~ store** पुस्तक की दुकान *pustak kee dukaan*

book, to बुक करना *book kurnaa*

booked up, to be बुक हो चुका *book ho chukaa*

booklet of tickets टिकटों की एक पुस्तिका *tickton kee ek pustak*

boots जूता *jota*

boring विनोदहीन *vinodheen*

born: I was born in जन्म लेना: मैने ... में जन्म लिया *janam lena: maine...main janam liya*

borrow: may I borrow your? उधार लेना: क्या मैं आपका उधार ले सकता हूँ? *udhaar lena: kya main aapkaa udhaar le saktaa hoon?*

botanical garden बोटा. निकल गार्डेन *botanical garden*

bottle बोतल *botal*; **~ of wine** मदिरा की बोतल *madira kee botal*; **~opener** बॉटल ऑपनर *bottle opener*

bottled बोतलबंद *botulbund*

bowel बोवल *bowel*

bowls कटोरा *katoraa*

box of chocolates चॉकलेट का डब्बा *choclate kaa dubba*

boy लड़का *ladkaa*

boyfriend पुरुष मित्र *purush mitr*

bra ब्रा *bra*

bracelet कंगन *kungun*

bread ब्रेड *bread*

bread: loaf of ~ ब्रेड: ब्रेड का लोफ *bread: bread kaa loaf*

break, to तोड़ना *todnaa*

break down: the cooker has broken down खराब होना: कुकर खराब हो गया है *kharaab hona: cooker kharaab ho gaya hai*

breakdown खराब होना *kharaab hona*; **~ truck** ब्रेकडाउन ट्रक *breakdown truck*; **have a ~** खराब होना *kharaab hona*

breakfast नाश्ता *nashtaa*

breast स्तन *stun*

breathe, to सांस लेना *saana lena*

bridge पुल *pool*

briefs जांघिया *jaanghiya*

bring someone, to किसी को लाना *kissi ko laana*

Britain ब्रिटेन *britain*

British ब्रिटिश *british*

brochure विवरणिका *vivranikaa*

broken, to be टूटना *tootnaa*

bronchitis फेफड़े की सूजन *phephade kee soojan*

brooch जड़ाऊ पिन *jadaau pin*

brother भाई *bhai*

brown भूरा *bhoora*

browse, to ब्राउज करना *browse kurnaa*

bruise चोट *chot*

bucket बाल्टी *baltee*

Buddha बुद्ध *buddha*

building भवन *bhawan*

built, to be निर्मित होना *nirmit hona*

bulletin board बुलेटिन बोर्ड *bulletin board*

bureau de change मुद्रा विनिमय कार्यालय *mudra vinimay karayalaya*

burger बर्गर *burger*; **~ stand** बर्गर स्टैंड *burger stand*

burn जलना *julnaa*

bus बस *bus*; **~ route** बस रूट *bus route*; **~ station** बस स्टेशन *bus station*; **~ stop** बस स्टॉप *bus stop*

business व्यवसाय *vyavasaay*; **~ class** बिज़नेस श्रेणी *business shrenee*; **~ trip** कारा. बारी यात्रा *karobaari yatra*; **on ~** व्यवसाय में *vyavasaay mein*

busy व्यस्त *vyast*

butane gas ब्यूटेन गैस *butane gas*

butcher कसाईखाना *kasaaikhaana*

butter मक्खन *mukhan*

button बटन *button*

buy, to खरीदना *khareednaa*

by (near) के पास *ke paas* **(time)** तक *tuk-*; **~bus** बस द्वारा *bus dwaara*; **~ car** कार द्वारा *car dwaara*; **~**

ferry नौका द्वारा *nauka dwaara*; **~ plane** जहाज द्वारा *jahaaj dwaara*; **~ train** ट्रेन द्वारा *train dwaara*; **~ credit card** क्रेडिट कार्ड द्वारा *credit card dwaara*

bye! अलविदा! *alvidaa!*

C

cabin केबिन *cabin*

cable TV केबल टीवी *cable tv*

café कैफे *cafe*

cagoule केगूल *cagoule*

cake केक *cake*

calendar कैलेंडर *calendar*

call, to बात करना *baat karnaa* **~ collect** कॉल कलैक्ट *call collect*; **~ for someone** किसी के लिए कॉल *kissi ke liye call*

call the police! पुलिस को बुलाओ! *police ko bulaao*

called: to be called बुलाया गया: बुलाया गया *bulaaya gaya: bulaaya gaya*

camera कैमरा *camera*; **~ case** कैमरा का खोल *camera kaa khol*; **~ store** कैमरा की दुकान *camera kee dukan*

camp, to पड़ाव डालना *padaav daalnaa*

campbed कैंप बेड *campbed*

camping कैंपिंग *camping*

campsite कैंप स्थल *camp sthal*

can कैन *can;* **~ opener** कैन ओपनर *can opener*

Canada कनाडा *canada*

Canadian कनाडावासी *canadawaasi*

cancel, to निरस्त करें *nirast karen*

cancer कैंसर *cancer*

candles मोमबत्ती *mombatti*

candy मिठाई *mithai*

cap टोपी *topi*

car कार *car;* **~ ferry** कार फेरी *car ferry;* **~ park** कार पार्क *car park;* **~ rental [hire]** किराए की कार *kiraaye kee car; by* **~** कार द्वारा *car dwaara*

car (train compart-ment) कार *car*

carafe सुराही *suraahi*

caravan (trailer) केरावान *caravan*

cards ताश *taash*

careful: be careful! सावधान! सावधान रहें! *saavdhaan: saavdhaan rahen*

carpet कालीन *kaaleen*

carrier bag ढोने वाला बैग *dhone waala bag*

cart ट्राली *trolley*

carton डब्बा *dubba*

cases खोल *khol*

cash नकद *nakad;* **~ machine** नकद मशीन *nakad machine*

cash, to नकद पाना *nakad paana*

cashier [cash desk] कैशियर *cashier*

casino कैसिनो *casino*

castle किला *kila*

catch, to (bus) पकड़ना *pakadnaa*

cathedral चर्च *church*

Catholic कैथोलिक *catholic*

cave गुफा *gufaa*

CD सीडी *cd;* **~-player** सीडी प्लेयर *cd player*

cemetery कब्रिस्तान *kabristaan*

center of town शहर के मध्य *sheher ke madhya*

central heating सेंट्रल हीटिंग *central heating*

ceramics सेरामिक *ceramic*

certificate प्रमाणपत्र *pramaan patra*

chain चेन *chain*

change (coins) बदलें *badlen*

change, to बदलें *badlen*

changing facilities बदलने की व्यवस्था *badalne kee vyavastha*

chapel गिरजाघर *girijaaghar*

charcoal लकड़ी का कोयला *lakdee kaa koylaa*

charge(s) शुल्क *shulk*

charter flight चार्टर उड़ान *charter udaan*

cheap सस्ता *sustaa*

cheaper और सस्ता *aur sustaa*

check book चेक बुक *check book*

check in, to चेक-इन करना *check-in kurnaa*

check-in desk चेक-इन डेस्क *check-in desk*

check out, to चेक-आउट करना *check-out karnaa*

checkout (supermar-ket) चेक-आउट *check-out*

cheers! मज़े करो! *maje karo*

cheese पनीर *paneer*

cheque book चेक बुक *check book*

chess (set) शतरंज (सेट) *shutranj (set)*

chest सीना *seena*

chewing gum च्यूइंग गम *chewing gum*

child बच्चा *buchha;* **~ seat** बच्चे की सीट *bucche kee seat*

children बच्चे *bucche;*

children's meals बच्चों का भोजन *bucche kaa bhojan*

chocolate चॉकलेट *choclate;* **~ bar** चा. कलेट बार *choclate bar;* **~ ice cream** आइसक्रीम चॉकलेट *choclate ice cream*

Christmas क्रिसमस *christmas*

church चर्च *church*

cigarette kiosk सिगरेट की दुकान *cigarette kee dukaan*

cigarettes, packet of सिगरेट का पैकेट *cigarette kaa packet*

cigars सिगार *cigar*

cinema सिनेमा *cinema*

claim check क्लेम चेक *claim check*

clean साफ *saaf*

clean, to साफ करना *saaf kurnaa*

cliff चट्टान *chatttan*

clinic चिकित्सालय *chikitsaalya*

cloakroom अमानती सामानघर *amaanee samaanghar*

clock घड़ी *ghadi*

close (near) नजदीक *najdeek*

close, to बंद करना *bund kurnaa*

clothes कपड़े *kapde;* **~ pins [pegs]** कपड़ों के लिए खूँटी *kapdon ke liye khoontee*

clothing store [clothes shop] कपड़ों की दुकान *kapdon kee dukaan*

cloudy, to be बदली होना *badlee hona*

clubs (golf) क्लब *club*

coach कोच *coach;* **~ station** कोच स्टेशन *coach station*

coast किनारा *kinaara*

coat कोट *coat;* **~ check** अमानती सामानघर *amaantee samaanghar;* **~ hanger** कोट हैंगर *coat hanger*

cockroach तिलचट्टा *tilchatta*

code (area, dialling) कोड (एरिया डायलिंग) *code (area dialing)*

coffee कॉफी *coffee*

coin सिक्का *sikka*

cold *(adj.)* ठंडा *thunda*

cold (flu) सर्दी (फ्लू) *sardee (flu)*

collapse: he's collapsed बेहोश होना: वह बेहोश हो गया *behosh hona: weh behosh ho gaya*

collect, to जमा करना *jama kurna*

color रंग *rang*; **~ film** रंगीन फिल्म *rangeen film*

comb कंघी *kunghee*

come back, to वापस आना *vaapus aana*

commission कमीशन *commission*

compact camera का. ॅम्पेक्ट कैमरा *compact camera*

compact disc कॉम्पेक्ट डिस्क *compact disc*

company (business) कंपनी *compani* (companionship) साथ *saath*

compartment (train) कंपार्टमेंट *compartment*

composer संगीतकार *sangeetkaar*

computer कंप्यूटर *computer*

concert संगीत-समारोह *sangeet samaroh*; **~ hall** संगीत-समारोह हॉल *sangeet-samaroh hall*

concession रिआयत *riyaaut*

concussion: he has ~ रिआयत: उसके पास रिआयत है *riyaaut: uske paas riyaaut hai*

conditioner कंडीशनर *conditioner*

condoms कंडोम *condom*

conductor कंडक्टर *conductor*

confirm, to निश्चित करें *nishchit karen*

congratulations! मुबारक! *mubaark*

connection संपर्क *sampark*

constipation कब्ज *kabz*

consulate कानस्युलेट *consulate*

consult, to परामर्श करना *paramash karnaa*

contact lens कॉन्टैक्ट लेंस *contact lens*

contact, to संपर्क करना *sampark kurnaa*

contagious, to be संक्रामक होना *sunkraamak hona*

contain, to रखना *rukhnaa*

contemporary dance समकालीन नृत्य *samkaaleen nritya*

contraceptive गर्भ नि. रोधक *garbh nirodhuk*

cook (n.) रसोइया *rasoiyaa* (v.) खाना बनाना *khaana banana*

cooker कुकर *cooker*

cookies बिस्कुट *biscuit*

cooking खाना बनाना *khanaa banana*

coolbox कूल बॉक्स *coolbox*

copper तांबा *tambaa*

copy नकल *nakal*

corkscrew कॉर्क स्क्रू *cork screw*

corner कोना *kona*

correct ठीक *theek*

cosmetics सौंदर्य प्रसाधन *saundarya prasadhan*

cot (child's) बिछौना *bichonaa*

cottage कुटिया *kutiyaa*

cotton [cotton wool] कॉटन *cotton*

cough खांसी *khaansee*

cough, to खांसना *khaansnaa*

country (nation) देश *desh*

country music लोक संगीत *lok sangeet*

course कोर्स *course*

cousin कज़न *cousin*

cover charge कवर शुल्क *cover shulk*

cow गाय *gaay*

craft shop शिल्पकला की दुकान *shilpkala kee dukaan*

cramps ऐंठन *ainthen*

credit card क्रेडिट कार्ड *credit card*; **~ number** नंबर *number*

crib पालना *paalnaa*

crisps कुरकुरे *kurkurre*

crockery क्रॉकरी *crockery*

cross क्रॉस *cross*

cross, to पार करना *paar kurnaa*

crossroad चौराहा *chauraahaa*

crowded भीड़ भाड़ *bheedbhaad*

crown (dental) क्राउन *crown*

cruise (n.) क्रूज़ *cruise*

crutches बैसाखी *baisaakhi*

crystal क्रिस्टल *crystal*

cuisine व्यंजन *vyunjun*

cup प्याला *pyalaa*

cupboard अलमारी *almari*

currency मुद्रा *mudra*; **~ exchange office** मुद्रा विनिमय कार्यालय *mudraa vinimay karayalaya*

curry करी *kari*

curtains परदा *purdaa*

customer service ग्राहक सेवा *grahak sewa*

customs सीमाशुल्क *seemashulk*; **~ declaration** घोषणापत्र *seemashulk ghoshnaa patra*

cut काटना *kaatnaa*; **~ and blowdry** कट और ब्लो ड्राइ *cut aur blow dry*

cutlery छुरी-कांटा *choori-kaanta*

cycle route साइकिल रास्ता *cycle raasta*

cycling साइकिल चालन *cycle challan*

D

daily प्रतिदिन *pratidin*

damaged, to be क्षतिग्र. ्स्त होना *shatigrast hona*

damp नमी *nami*

dance (n.) नृत्य *nritya*

dancing, to go नृत्य के लिए जाना *nritya ke liye jaana*

dangerous खतरनाक *khatarnaak*

dark अंधेरा *ndheraa*

daughter बेटी *beti*

dawn उषा काल *usha kaal*

day दिन *din*; **~ ticket** दिन का टिकट *din kaa ticket*; **~ trip** दिन की यात्रा *din kee yatra*

dead (battery) मृत (बैटरी) *mrit (battery)*

deaf, to be बहरा होना *behraa hona*

December दिसम्बर *disambar*

deck chair डेक कुर्सी *deck kursee*

declare, to घोषणा करना *ghoshnaa kurnaa*

deduct, to घटाना *ghataana*

deep गहरा *gehraa*; **~ freeze** डीप फ्रीज *deep freeze*

defrost, to डिफ़ॉस्ट करना *defrost kurnaa*

degrees डिग्री *degree*

delay देरी *deri*

delicatessen तैयार खाने की दुकान *tayaar khaane kee dukaan*

delicious स्वादिष्ट *swadisht*

deliver, to सौंपना *saupnaa*

denim डेनिम *denim*

dental floss डेंटल फ़्लॉस *dental floss*

dentist दंत विशेषज्ञ *dunt visheshagay*

dentures दन्तावली *dantawali*

deodorant डिओडेंट *deodorant*

depart, to छूटना *chootnaa*

department विभाग *vibhaag*; **~ store** डिपार्टमेंट स्टोर *department store*

departure lounge प्रत्यान विश्राम-कक्ष *prasthan vishraam kaksha*

deposit (security) जमाराशि *jamaraashi*

describe, to विवरण देना *vivrun dena*

destination गंतव्य *gantavaya*

details विस्तृत *vistrit*

detergent डिटरजेंट *detergent*

develop, to (photos) विकसित करना *viksit kurnaa*

diabetes मधुमेह *madhumeh*

diabetic, to be मधुमेह का रोगी होना *mad-humeh kaa rogi hona*

diagnosis रोग-निदान *rog-nidaan*

diamond हीरा *heera*

diapers डायपर *diaper*

diarrhea दस्त *dust*; **I have ~** मुझे दस्त है *mujhe dust hai*

dice पांसा *paansaa*

dictionary शब्दकोश *shabdkosh*

diesel डीजल *diesel*

diet: I'm on a diet डाइट: मैं डाइट पर हूँ *diet: main diet pur hoon*

difficult मुश्किल *mushkil*

dining: ~ car डाइनिंग: डाइनिंग कार *dianing: dianing car*; **~ room** भोजनकक्ष *bhojankak-sh* **dinner: to have ~** रात का भोजन: रात का भोजन करना *raat kaa bhojan:raat kaa bhojan*; **~ jacket** डाइनिंग जैकेट *dianing jacket*

direct सीधा *seedha*

direction, in the... of दिशा, ... की दिशा में *deesha...deshaa mein*

directions दिशाएं *dishayen*

director (of company) निर्देशक *nirdeshak*

directory (telephone) डायरेक्ट्री *directory*

dirty गंदा *gundaa*

disabled (n.) विकलांग *viklaang*

discotheque डिस्को *disco*

discount छूट *chhoot*

dish व्यंजन *vyunjun*; **~ cloth** गुड़िया क्लॉथ *dish cloth*

dishwashing liquid बर्तन धुलाई के लिए द्रव *bartan dhulaai ke liye drawye*

dislocated, to be सरक जाना *sadak jaana*

display cabinet/case प्रदर्शन केबिनेट/केस *pradarshan cabinet/case*

disposable camera डिस्पोनेबल कैमरा *disposable camera*

distilled water डिस्टिल्ड पानी *distilled paani*

disturb: don't disturb परेशान करना: कृपया परेशान ना करें *pareeshaan karnaa: kripyaa pareeshaan naa karen*

dive, to कूदना *koodnaa*

diversion (detour) मोड़ *mod*

diving equipment गोताखोरी उपकरण *gotakhori upkaran*

divorced, to be तलाकशुदा होना *talaakshudaa hona*

dizzy: I feel dizzy चक्कर आना: मुझे चक्कर आ रहा है *chakkar aana: mujhe chakkar aa raha hai*

do: things to ~ करना: करने योग्य कार्य *karna: karne yogya karyaa;*

what do you do? आप क्या करते हैं? *aap kya karte hain;*

do you accept ...? क्या आप ... स्वीकार करते हैं? *kya aap ... sweekaar karte hain;*

do you have ...? क्या आपके पास ... है *kya aapke paas ... hai*

doctor चिकित्सक *chikitsak*

doesn't work काम नहीं करता *kaam nahin kurtaa*

doll गुड़िया *gudiyaa*

dollar डॉलर *dollar*

door द्वार *dwaar*

double डबल *double;* **~ bed** डबल बेड *double bed* **~ room** डबल रूम *double room*

downstairs निचली मंजिल *nichlee manzil*

downtown area डाउन. टाउन क्षेत्र *downtown shetre*

dozen दर्जन *darzan*

draft [draught] (beer) ड्राफ्ट *draft*

dress कपड़े *kapde*

drink (n.) ड्रिंक *drink*

drinking water पीने का पानी *peene kaa paani*

drip, to: the faucet [tap] drips टपकना: टोंटी टपक रही है *apaknaa: toontee tapak rahi hai*

drive, to चलाना *chalana*

driver ड्राइवर *driver*

driver's license ड्राइवर का लाइसेंस *driver ka license*

drop someone off, to किसी को छोड़ना *kissi ko chodnaa*

drowning: someone is drowning डूबना: कोई डूब रहा है *doobnaa: koi doob raha hai*

drugstore दवाख़ाना *dawakhaana*

drunk नशे में चूर *nashe mein choor*

dry cleaner ड्राई क्लिनर *dry cleaner*

dry-clean, to ड्राई क्लीन करना *dry clean kurnaa*

dubbed, to be डब करना *dub kurnaa*

during दौरान *dauraan*

dustbins कूड़े का डब्बा *koodhe kaa dubba*

duty: to pay duty ड्यूटी: ड्यूटी देना *duty: duty dena*

duvet रजाई *rajaai*

E

e-mail ई-मेल *e-mail; ~* **address** ई-मेल पता *e-mail pata*

ear कान *kaan; ~* **drops** कान की दवाई *kaan kee dawaai; ~* **ache** कान का दर्द *kaan kaa dard*

early जल्दी *jaldee*

earlier पहले *pehlee*

earrings झुमका *jhumkaa*

east पूरब *purub*

Easter ईस्टर *easter*

easy आसान *aasaan*

eat, to भोजन करना *bhojan kurnaa*

economy class इका. नॉमी श्रेणी *economy shreni*

eggs अंडे *unde*

elastic *(adj.)* इलास्टिक *elastic*

electric: ~ shaver बि. जली: इलेक्ट्रिक शेवर *bijlee: electric shaver*

electrical outlets बिजली का निकास बिंदु *bijlee kaa nikaas bindu*

electricity meter बिजली मीटर *bijlee meter*

electronic: ~ flash इलेक्ट्रॉनिक इलेक्ट्रॉनिक फ़्लैश *electronic: electronic flash; ~* **game** इलेक्ट्रॉनिक खेल *electronic khel; ~* **items** इलेक्ट्रॉनिक वस्तु *electronic vustu*

elephant हाथी *haathi*

elevator लिफ़्ट *lift*

else: something else अन्य: कुछ और *anya: kuch aur*

email ईमेल *email*

embassy दूतावास *dootavaas*

emerald पन्ना *punna*

emergency आपातक. ालीन *aapaatkaleen*

emergency exit आपातकालीन निकास *aapaatkaleen nikaas*

empty ख़ाली *khaali*

enamel इनामेल *enamel*

end, to ख़त्म करना *khatam kurnaa*

end: at the end अंत: अंत में *ant: ant mein*

engaged, to be व्यस्त होना *vyast hona*

engine इंजन *engine*

engineering इंजीनियरिंग *engineering*

England इंग्लैंड *england*

English अंग्रेज़ *angrez~~* **speaking** अंग्रेज़ी बोलने वाला *angreji bolne waala*

enjoy, to आनंद लेना *anand lena*

enlarge, to बड़ा करना *bada karna*

enough पर्याप्त *paryapt; that's ~* बहुत हो गया *bahut ho gaya*

entertainment guide मनोरंजन गाइड *manoranjan guide*

entrance fee प्रवेश शुल्क *pravesh shulk*

entry visa प्रवेश वीसा *pravesh visa*

envelope लिफ़ाफ़ा *lifafa*

epileptic, to be मिरगी का रोगी होना *mirgee kaa rogee hona*

equipment *(sports)* उपकरण *upkaran*

error दोष *dosh*

escalator एक्सकेलेटर *escalator*

essential आवश्यक *aavashyak*

E.U. *(European Union)* ई. यू. (यूरोपीय संघ) *E.U. (european sangh)*

evening: in the ~ शाम: शाम में *shaam: shaam mein; ~* **dress** शाम के कपड़े *shaam ke kapde*

events कार्यक्रम *karyakaram*

every: ~ day प्रत्येक: प्रतिदिन *pratyek: pratidin; ~* **hour** प्रति घंटा *prati ghanta; ~* **week** प्रति सप्ताह *prati suptaah*

examination *(medical)* जाँच *jaanch*

example, for उदाहरण तत्या *udharantya*

except सिवाय *sivaay*

excess baggage बहुतायात सामान *bahutayat samaan*

exchange, to अदला-बदली *adlaa-badlee ~* **rate** विनिमय दर *vinimay dur*

excluding meals भोजन के बिना *bhojan ke bina*

excursion साहसिक यात्रा *shasik yatra*

excuse me *(attention)* कृपया ध्यान दें *kripya dhyaan dein*

excuse me? (pardon?) माफ़ कीजिएगा? *maaf kijiyegaa*

exit निकास *nikaas*

expected, to be आशंवित रहना *ashanchit rehnaa*

expensive महंगा *mehengaa*

expiration [expiry] date एक्सपाइरी तिथि *expiry tithi*

exposure *(photos)* एक्सपोजर *exposure*

express व्यस्त करना *vyakt karna*

extension एक्सटेंशन *extension*

extra अतिरिक्त *atirikt*

extracted, to be *(tooth)* उखड़वाना *ukhaadvaana*
eye आंख *aankh*

F

fabric वस्त्र *vastra*
face चेहरा *chehra*
facial फ़ेशियल *facial*
facilities व्यवस्था *vyavustha*
factor (sun cream) फ़ैक्टर *factor*
faint, to feel बेहोशी महसूस करना *behhoshi mehsoos kurnaa*
fall (season) पतझड़ *putjhad*
family परिवार *parivaar*
famous प्रसिद्ध *praseedh*
fan पंखा *pankha*
far दूर *door;* --**sighted** दूर- दृष्टि *door-drishti;*
how far is it? यह कितनी दूर है? *yeh kitni door pur hai?*
fare किराया *kiraya*
farm खेत *khet*
fast फ़ास्ट *fast;* ~ **food** फ़ूड *food;* ~ **food restaurant** फ़ास्ट-शाम रेस्टोरेंट *fast-food restaurant*
fast, to be (clock) तेज़ होना (घड़ी) *tej, hona (ghaadi)*
fat चर्बी *churbee*
father पिता *pita*
faucet नल *nul*
faulty: this is faulty ख़राब: यह ख़राब है*kharaab: yeh kharaab hai*
favorite पसंदीदा *pasandeeda*
fax machine फ़ैक्स मशीन *fax machine*

February फ़रवरी *furvari*
feed, to खाना खिलाना *khaana khilaana*
feeding bottle फ़ीडिंग बोतल *feeding bottle*
feel ill, to बीमार महसूस करना *bimaar mehsoos kurnaa*
female महिला *mahilaa*
ferry फ़ेरी *ferry*
feverish, to feel बुख़ार महसूस करना *bukhaar mehsoos kurnaa*
few थोड़ा *thodaa*
fiancé(e) मंगेतर *mangetur*
field मैदान *maidaan*
fifth पांचवां *panchwaa*
fight लड़ाई *ladaai*
fill out, to भरें *bharen*
filling (dental) भराई *bharaai*
film फ़िल्म *film*
filter फ़िल्टर *filter*
find, to खोजना *yojnaa*
fine (n.) जुर्माना *jurmaana*
fine (adj.) अच्छा *acha*
finger अंगुली *unglee*
fire: ~ **alarm** अग्नि: अग्नि अलार्म *agnee: agnee alarm;* ~ **department [brigade]** अग्नि विभाग *agnee vibhaag* ~ **escape** अग्नि से बचाव *agnee se bachav;* ~ **extinguisher** अग्नि शामक *agnee shaamak*
there's a fire! यहाँ आग है! *wahan aag hai!*
firewood जरावन *jaravan*
first प्रथम *pratham;* ~ **class** (ticket) प्रथम श्रेणी (टिकट) *pratham shreni (ticket)*

fish restaurant मछली रेस्टोरेंट *uchlee restaurant*
fish store [fishmonger] मछली की दुकान *muchlee kee dukaan*
fit, to फ़िट होना *fit hona*
fitting room फ़िटिंग रूम *fitting room*
fix, to दुरुस्त करना *durust kurnaa*
flashlight फ़्लैश लाइट *flash light*
flat (puncture) पंचर *puncture*
flavor: what flavors do you have? स्वाद: आपके पास कौन सा स्वाद है? *swaad: aapke paas kaun sa swaad hai?*
flea पिस्सू *pissu*
flight उड़ान *udaan;* ~ **number** उड़ान संख्या *udaan sankhya*
flip-flops फ़्लिप-फ़्लॉप *flip-flop*
floor (level) फ़र्श *fursh*
florist फूल विक्रेता *phooln vikretaa*
flour आटा *aataa*
flower फूल *phool*
flu फ़्लू *flu*
flush: the toilet won't flush फ़्लश: टॉयलेट में फ़्लश नहीं चल रहा। *flush: toilet mein flush nahin chul raha*
fly (insect) मक्खी *mukhi*
foggy, to be कोहरेदार होना *kohredaar hona*
folk art लोक-कला *lok kala*
folk music लोक-संगीत *lok-sangeet*

follow, to अनुकरण करना *anukaran karnaa*
food भोजन *bhojan;* ~ **poisoning** विषैले भोजनपान की बीमारी *vishella bhojanpaan ki beemari*
foot पैर *pair;* ~ **path** पगडंडी *pugdundee*
football फ़ुटबॉल *football*
for के लिए *ke liye;* ~ **a day** एक दिन के लिए *ek din ke liye;* ~ **a week** एक सप्ताह के लिए *ek saptaah ke liye*
forecast पूर्वानुमान *purvanamaan*
foreign currency विदेशी मुद्रा *videshi mudra*
forest जंगल *jungle*
forget, to भुल जाना *bhool jaana*
fork कांटा *kaanta*
form फ़ॉर्म *form*
formal dress नियमानुसार कपड़े *niyamnusaar kapde*
fortnight पाक्षिक *paakshik*
fortunately सौभाग्यवश *saubhagyavash*
fountain फ़व्वारा *phavaaraa*
four-door car चार दरवाज़े वाली कार *chaar durwaaje waali car*
four-wheel drive व्हील ड्राईव *four wheel drive*
fourth चतुर्थ *chaturth*
foyer फ़ॉएर *foyer*
fracture फ़्रेक्चर *fracture*
frame (glasses) फ़्रेम *frame*

free फ्री *free*

freezer फ्रीज़र *freezer*

frequent: how frequent? आवृति: कितनी बार? *aavriti: kitni baar?*

frequently अक्सर *aksar*

fresh ताज़ा *fresh*

Friday शुक्रवार *shukravaar*

fried तले हुआ *tale hua*

friend मित्र *mitr*

friendly मित्रतापूर्वक *mitrataapurvak*

fries फ्राई *fries*

frightened, to be डर जाना *dur jaana*

from (come from) से *se*

front सामने *saamne;* **~ door** सामने का द्वार *saamne ka dwaar*

frosty, to be पालेदार होना *paaledaar hona*

frying pan तलने के लिए बर्तन *talne ke liye bartan*

fuel इंधन *indhun*

full पूर्ण *purun;* **~ board** (American Plan [A.P.]) पूर्ण भोजन *purun bhojan* **~ insurance** पूर्ण बीमा *purun beema*

fun, to have मस्ती करना *masti karma*

furniture फर्नीचर *furniture*

further और *aur*

fuse फ्यूज़ *fuse;* **~ box** फ्यूज़ बॉक्स *fuse box*

G

gallon गैलन *gallon*

game (soccer, etc.) खेल *khel*

game (toy) खेल *khel*

garage गैराज *garage*

garbage bags कूड़े की थैली *koode kee theli*

garden बगीचा *bageecha*

gas: I smell gas! गैस: मुझे गैस की गंध आ रही है! *gas: mujhe gas ki gundh aa rahi hai;* **~ bottle** गैस की बोतल *gas ki botal*

gas station गैस स्टेशन *gas station*

gasoline गैसोलीन *gasoline*

gate (airport) द्वार *dwaar*

gauze बैंडेज *bandage*

gay club समलैंगिक क्लब *sumlaingik club*

genuine असली *aslee*

get, to पाना *paana* **~ off** चले जाओ *chalo jao;* **~ to** (reach) पहुंचो *pahooncho;*

how do I get to? मैं … तक कैसे पहुँचुंगा? *main...tuk kaise pahoonchugaa*

gift उपहार *uphaar;* **~ store** उपहार की दुकान *uphaar ki dukaan*

girl लड़की *ladki*

girlfriend महिला मित्र *mahila mitr*

give, to देना *dena*

give way (yield) रास्ता देना *rastaa dena*

gland ग्रन्थि *granthi*

glass गिलास *gilaas*

glasses (optical) चश्मा *chushma*

glossy finish चमकीली फिनिश *chumkeela finish*

glove दस्ताना *dustaana*

go: to ~ to जाओ: पर जाओ *jao: pur jao*

let's ~! चलें चलें! *chalo chalen;* **~ away!** दूर चले जाओ! *door chale jao*

goggles धूप का चश्मा *dhoop ka chushma*

gold सोना *sona;* **~-plate** सोने का प्लेट *sone ka plate*

golf गोल्फ़ *golf;* **~ course** गोल्फ़ कोर्स *golf course*

good अच्छा *acha-* **morning** सुप्रभात *suprabhaat;* **~ after-noon** नमस्ते *namaste;* **~ evening** नमस्ते *namaste;* **~ night** शुभरात्रि *shubhratri;* **~ value** अच्छा मूल्य *acha mulya-* **bye** नमस्ते *namaste*

gram (weight) ग्राम *gram*

grandparents (paternal) दादा-दादी /(maternal) नाना-नानी *dada-dadi/ nana-nani*

grapes अंगूर *angoor*

grass घास *ghaas*

gray भूरा *bhoora*

graze (cut) खरोंच *kharonch*

great (excellent) बहुत बढ़िया *bahut badhiyaa*

great (good idea) महान *mahaan*

green हरा *hara*

greengrocer सब्जियों की दुकान *subjeeyon kee dukaan*

grilled ग्रिल्ड *grilled*

grocer किराने की दुकान *kiraane ki dukaan*

ground (earth) ज़मीन *zameen;* **~ cloth [~sheet]** पोछा *poucha*

group समूह *samooh*

guarantee गारंटी *guarantee*

guide (tour) गाइड *guide*

guidebook स्थान सूचक पुस्तक *sthan soochak pustak*

guided tour मार्ग-दर्शित भ्रमण *marg-darshit bhraman*

guided walk/hike मार्ग-दर्शित पैदल चालन/सैर *marg-darshit paidal/chaalan*

guitar गिटार *guitar*

gum गोंद *gond*

guy rope रस्सी *russi*

gynecologist स्त्री रोग विशेषज्ञ *stree rog visheshyagya*

H

hair बाल *baal;* **~ mousse/gel** हेयर मूस/जेल *hair mousse/ gel;* **~ spray** हेयर स्प्रे *hair spray;* **~ cut** बाल कटाई *baal kataai*

hairdresser हेयर डेसर *hair dresser*

hammer हथौड़ा *hathodaa*

hand हाथ *haath;* **~ luggage** हैंडबैग *handbag;* **~ washable** हाथ से धोने योग्य *haath se dhone yogya*

handbag हैंडबैग *handbag*

handicapped, to be पंगु होना *pungu hona*

handicrafts हस्तशिल्प *hasthshilp*

handkerchief रूमाल *rumaal*

hanger हैंगर *hanger*

hangover हैंगओवर *hangover*

happy: I'm not happy with the service खुश: मैं सेवा से खुश नहीं हूँ *khush: main sewa se khush nahin hoon*

harbor बंदरगाह *bandargaah*

hat हैट *hat*

have है *hai*

can I have? क्या मुझे मिल सकता है? *kya mujhe mil saktaa hai–*

to क्या मुझे करना ज़रूरी है *kya mujhe kurna zaroori hai;* **an appointment** क्या मुझे अपॉयन्टमेंट मिल सकता है *kya mujhe appointment mil sakti hai*

hayfever बुखार *bukhaar*

head मुख्य *mukhya;* **waiter** मुख्य वेटर *mukhya waiter* **ache** सिर दर्द *sir dard*

heading, to be बढ़ना *badna*

health food store हेल्थ फूड स्टोर *health food store*

hear, to सुनना *sunna*

hearing aid हिअरिंग ऐड *hearing aid*

heart हृदय *hridya;* **attack** दिल का दौरा *dil kaa daura;* **condition** हृदय रोग *hridya rog*

hearts *(cards)* पान *paan*

heater हीटर *heater*

heating गर्म करना *garm karnaa*

heavy भारी *bhaari*

height ऊंचाई *unchaai*

hello नमस्ते *namaste*

help: can you help me? सहायता: क्या आप मेरी सहायता कर सकते हैं? *sahaytaa: kya aap meri sahaytaa kur sakte hain*

hemorrhoids बवासीर *bawasir*

her उसकी *uski*

here यहाँ *yahan*

hernia हर्निया *hernia*

hers उसका *uskaa;* **it's hers** यह उसका है *yeh uska hai*

hi! नमस्ते! *namaste*

high उच्च *ucch*

highlight, to (hair) हाईलाईट करना *highlight kurna*

highway हाइवे *highway*

hike *(n.)* सैर *sair*

hiking सैर *sair;* **boots** सैर करने वाला जूता *sair karne waala jota*

hill पहाड़ी *pahadi*

hire, to किराए ij ysuk *kiraye pur lena*

his उसका *uska;* **it's his** यह उसका है *yeh uska hai*

hitchhiking लिफ्ट मांगना *lift mangnaa*

HIV-positive एच आइ वी-पॉज़िटिव *HIV-positive*

hobby शौक *shauk*

hold on, to पकड़े रहना *pakde rehnaa*

hole छिद्र *chidr*

holiday: on छुट्टी: छुट्टी पर *chutti: chutti pur;* **resort** हॉलिडे रिसॉर्ट *holiday resort*

home: we're going home घर: हमलोग घर जा रहे हैं *ghar: hum log jaa rahen hain*

homosexual समलैंगिक *sumlaingik*

honeymoon: we're on honeymoon हनीमून: हम लोग हनीमून पर हैं *honeymoon: hum log honeymoon pur hain*

hopefully आशापूर्वक *aashapurvak*

horse घोड़ा *ghodaa;* **racing** घुड़दौड़ *ghuddaud*

hospital अस्पताल *aspataal*

hot गर्म *garm;* **dog** हॉट डॉग *hot dog;* **spring** गर्म सोता *garm sota* **water** गर्म पानी *garm paani*

hotel होटल *hotel*

hour घंटा *ghuntaa;* **in an** एक घंटे में *ek ghunte mein*

house घर *ghar*

housewife गृहिणी *grahini*

hovercraft हॉवर क्राफ्ट *hover craft*

how? कैसे? *kaise*

how are you? आप कैसे हैं? *aap kaise hain*

how far...? कहां तक ...? *kahan tuk...*

how long...? कब तक ...? *kub tuk...*

how many...? कितनी बार ...? *kitnee baar...*

how much? *(money)* कितने? *kitne*

how much? *(quantity)* कितनी? *kitnee*

how often? कितनी बार? *kitnee baar*

how old? कितना पुराना? *kitnaa puranna*

hundred सौ *sau;* **thousand** लाख *lakh*

hungry: I'm hungry भूखा होना: मैं भूखा हूँ *bhook hona: main bhookha hoon*

hurry: I'm in a hurry जल्दी: मैं जल्दी में हूँ *jaldee: main jaldee mein hoon*

hurt, to चोट पहुंचाना *chot pahoonchnaa;* **my mera** मेरा *mera;* **hurts:** दर्द *dard kurta hai;* **to be hurt** चोट *gksuk chot hona*

husband पति *pati*

I'd like मैं पसंद करूंगा *main pasand karoonga*

I'll have मैं लूंगा *main loonga*

ice बर्फ *burf*

ice cream आइसक्रीम *ice cream;* **parlor** आइसक्रीम पार्लर *ice cream parlour*

icy, to be बर्फीला होना *burfeela hona*

identification पहचान *pehchaan*

ill: I'm ill बीमार: मैं बीमार हूँ *bimaar: main bimaar hoon*

illegal: is it illegal? गैरकानूनी: यह गैरक. नूनी है? *gair kanooni: yeh gair kanooni hai*

imitation नकल *nakal*

immediately तुरंत *turunt*

in में *mein*

included: is included? शामिल: क्या यह शामिल है? *shaamil: kya yeh shaamil hai*

India भारत *bharat*

indicate, to दर्शाना *durshaana*

indigestion बदहजमी *badhhazmee*

indoor pool इंडोर पूल *indoor pool*

inexpensive सस्ता *sustaa*

infected, to be संक्रमित होना *sankraamit hona*

infection संक्रमण *sankraman*

inflammation of की जलन *kee zalan*

informal अनौपचारिक *anopchaareek*

information सूचना *soochnaa*; ~ **desk** सूचना डेस्क *soochnaa desk*; ~ **office** सूचना कार्यालय *soochnaa karalaya*

Information (telephone service) सूचना *soochnaa*

injection सुई *sui*

injured, to be घायल होना *ghayal hona*

innocent नादान *naadaan*

insect कीड़ा *keera*; ~

bite कीड़े का काटना *keere kaa kaatnaa*; ~ **repellent** कीड़ा भगाने वाला *keera bhagane waala*

inside अंदर *andar*

insist: I insist दृढ़ होना: मैं दृढ़ हूँ *dridh hona: main dridh hoon*

insomnia नींद ना आने की बीमारी *neend naa aane kee bimaaree*

instant coffee इंस्टेंट कॉफी *instant coffee*

instead of सिवाय *siwaay*

instructions निर्देश *nirdesh*

instructor अध्यापक *adhyapak*

insulin इंसुलिन *insulin*

insurance बीमा *beema*; ~ **card** बीमा कार्ड *bema card*; ~ **claim** बीमा दावा *bema dawa*

interest (hobby) रुचि *ruchi*

interesting रुचिकर *rucheekur*

International Student Card अंतर्राष्ट्रीय स्टुड. ेंट कार्ड *anturrashtriya student card*

Internet इंटरनेट *internet*

interpreter अनुवादक *anuvaaduk*

intersection चौराहे *chaurahe*

introduce oneself, to अपना परिचय दें *apnaa parichay dein*

invitation आमंत्रण *aamantran*

invite, to आमंत्रित करें *aamantrit karen*

involved, to be शामिल होना *shaamil hona*

iodine आयोडिन *iodine*

Ireland आयरलैंड *Ireland*

Irish आयरिश *irish*

is: is it? है: है कि नहीं? *hai: hai ki nahin*

is there? क्या है? *kya*

is this? क्या यह? *kya yeh*

it is यह है *yeh hai*

Italian (cuisine) इतलवी *itaalvee*

itch: it itches खुजली: यह खुजलाता है *khujlee: yeh khujultaa hai*

itemized bill आइटमड. इज्ड बिल *itemized bill*

J

jacket जैकेट *jacket*

jam जैम *jam*

jammed, to be जाम होना *jaam hona*

January जनवरी *janvari*

Japan जापान *japan*

Japanese जापानी *japanee*

jar डब्बा *dubba*

jaw जबड़ा *jubdaa*

jazz जैज *jazz*

jeans जींस *jeans*

jellyfish जेलीफिश *jellyfish*

jet lag: I'm jet lagged जेट लैग: मुझे जेट लैग है *jet lag: mujhe jet lag hai*

jet-ski जेट स्की *jet ski*

jeweler जौहरी *johree*

joke मजाक *majaak*

journalist पत्रकार *patrakaar*

journey यात्रा *yatraa*

jug (of water) जग *jug*

July जुलाई *july*

jump leads जंप लीड्स *jump leads*

jumper जंपर *jumper*

junction (intersection) जंक्शन *junction*

June जून *june*

K

keep: keep the change! रखें: खुल्ले रख लीजिए! *rakhen: khulle rukh lijiye*

kerosene किरासिन *kerosene*; ~ **stove** किरासिन का चूल्हा *kerosene kaa chulhaa*

ketchup केचप *ketchup*

kettle केतली *ketlee*

key चाबी *chaabee*; ~ **ring** चाबी का गुच्छा *chaabee kaa guchha*

kiddie pool खेलने के लिए छोटा तालाब *khelne ke liye chota talaab*

kidney गुर्दा *gurdaa*

kilogram किलोग्राम *kilogram*

kilometer किलोमीटर *kilometer*

kind (pleasant) सुहाना *suhana*

kind: what kind of प्रकार: किस प्रकार का *prakaar: kis prakaar kaa*

kiss, to चुंबन लेना *chumbun lena*

kitchen रसोईघर *rasoi ghar*

knapsack झोला *jhola*

knee घुटना *ghutnaa*
knickers निकर्स *knickers*
knife चाकू *chaaku*
know: I don't know
जानना: मैं नहीं जानता
jaannaa: main nahin jaantaa
Korea कोरिया *korea*
Korean कोरियाई *koreaai*
kosher कोशर *kosher*

L
label लेबल *label*
lace फीता *pheeta*
ladder सीढ़ी *seedhe*
lake झील *jheel*
lamp लैंप *lamp*
land, to उतरना *uturnaa*
language course भाषा कोर्स *bhasha course*
large बड़ा *bada*
larger ज्यादा बड़ा *jyadaa bada*
last अंतिम *anteem*
last, to समाप्त होना *samapt hona*
late देर (देरी होना) *der (deri hona)*
later बाद में *baad mein*
laugh, to हंसना *hansnaa*
laundromat लॉन्ड्रोमैट *Laundromat*
laundry: ~ facilities
कपड़ा धुलाई: कपड़ा धुलाई व्यवस्था *kapdaa dhulaai: kapdaa dhulaai vyavustha;* **~ service** कपड़ा धुलाई सेवा *kapdaa dhulaai sewa*
lavatory प्रसाधन कक्ष *prasadhun kaksh*
lawyer वकील *vakeel*
laxative शिथिल करने वाला

sheetheel karne wala
lead, to (road) मार्ग दिखलाना *maarg dikhlana*
leader नेता *neta*
leak, to टपकना *tapaknaa*
learn, to सीखना *seekhnaa*
leather चमड़ा *chamdaa*
leave, to (deposit)
जमाराशि *jamaraashi (person)* छोड़ना *chhomaa (aircraft)* से जाना *se jaanaa*
leave me alone! मुझे अकेला छोड़ दो! *mujhe akelaa chhod do*
left: on the ~ बाएं: बाएं में *bayan: bayan mein*
left-luggage office
खोया सामान कार्यालय *khoya saaman karyalay*
leg पैर *pair*
legal: is it legal? कान. नी: क्या यह कानूनी है? *kanoonee: kya yeh kanoonee hai*
leggings लेगिंग्स *leggings*
lemon नींबू *neembu*
lemonade लेमोनेड *lemonade*
lend: could you lend me? उधार देना: क्या आप मुझे उधार दे सकते हैं? *udhaar dena: kya aap mujhe udhaar de sakte hain*
length (of) लंबाई (का) *lumbaai (kaa)*
lens लेंस *lens* **~ cap** लेंस कैप *lens cap*
lesbian club लेस्बियन क्लब *lesbian club*

less कम *kum*
lesson पाठ *path*
let: let me know! करने देना: मुझे बताओ! *karne dena: mujhe batao*
letter पत्र *patra;* **~ box** पत्र पेटी *patra peti*
level (even ground) स्तर *stur*
library पुस्तकालय *pustakalaya*
lie down, to लेट जाना *let jaana*
lifeboat जीवन-रक्षक नौका *jeevan-rakshak nauka*
lifeguard जीवन-रक्षक *jeevan-rakshak*
lifejacket जीवन-रक्षक जैकेट *jeevan-rakshak jacket*
life preserver [belt] बेल्ट *belt*
lift (elevator) लिफ्ट *lift*
lift (hitchhiking) लिफ्ट लेना *lift lena*
light (electric) लाइट *light;* **~ bulb** लाइट बल्ब *light bulb* **~ color** हल्का *hulkaa* **~ weight** हल्का *hulkaa;*
lighter (color) ज्यादा हल्का *jyadaa hulka; (cigarette)* लाइटर *lighter*
like: ~ this समान: इसके समान *samaan: iske samaan*
like, to पसंद करना *pasand kurnaa*
I like it मैं पसंद करता हूँ *main pasand karta hoon*
I don't like it मैं पसंद नहीं करता हूँ *main pasand nahin kartaa hoon*

I'd like मैं पसंद करूंगा *main pasand karoongaa*
limousine लिमोज़िन *limousine*
line (subway [metro]) लाईन *line*
linen लिनेन *linen*
lip होंठ *honth;* **~ stick** लिपस्टिक *lipstick*
liqueur मीठी सुगन्धित शराब *meethi sugandhit sharaab*
liquor store शराब की दुकान *sharaab kee dukaan*
liter लीटर *liter*
little छोटा *chhota*
live, to जीना *jeena;* **~ together** साथ जीना *saath jeena*
liver कलेजा *kaleja*
living room लिविंग रूम *living room*
lobby लॉबी *lobby*
local स्थानीय *sthaniye* **~ anaesthetic** स्थानीय असंवेदनता की दवा *sthaniye asunvedantaa kee dawaa*
lock, to ~ oneself out बंद, अपने को बाहर बंद कर लेना *bund, apne ko baahar bund kur lena*
log on, to लॉग आन करना *log aan karnaa*
long लंबा *lambaa;* **~distance** लंबी दूरी *lambee doori;* **~sighted** दूर दृष्टि दोष *door drishti dosh;* **how long** कितना लंबा *kitnaa lumba*
look: I'm just looking देखो: मैं सिर्फ़ देख रहा हूँ *dekho: main sirf*

dekh raha hoon; **look like** समान दिखना *samaan dikhna;* **to be looking for** देखना लिए *dekhna liye*

loose ढीला *dheela*

lorry लॉरी *lorry*

lose, to ढीला करना *dheela karma*

I've lost मैं खो चुका हूँ *main kho chukka hoon*

lost-and-found office [lost property office] खोया-और-पाया कार्यालय *khoya aur paayaa karyalaya*

lots of fun बहुत सारा मज़ा *bahut saara maza*

louder ज़्यादा तेज़ आवाज़ *jyadaa tez aawaaz*

love: I love you प्यार: मैं तुम्हें प्यार करता हूँ *pyaar: main tumhe pyaar kurta hoon*

lovely प्यारा *pyaara*

low निम्न *nimn;* **~ bridge** नीचा पुल *neecha pul;* **~-fat** कम चर्बी *kum churbee*

luck: good luck भाग्य: सौभाग्य *bhagaya: saubhagaya*

luggage सामान *samaan;* **~ cart [trolley]** सामान की ट्राली *samaan ki trolley* **~ locker** अमानती सामानघर *amaantee samaanghar*

lump सूजन *soojun*

lunch दोपहर का भोजन *dopaher kaa bhojan*

lung फेफड़ा *phephdaa*

M

machine washable मशीन से धोने योग्य *machine se dhone yogya*

madam मैडम *madam*

magazine पत्रिका *patreekaa*

magnificent शानदार *shaandaar*

maid नौकरानी *naukraani*

mail [n.] चिट्ठी *chitthi;* **by-** चिट्ठी द्वारा *chitthi dwrara;* **~ box** पत्र पेटी *patra peti;* [v.] चिट्ठी भेजना *chitthi bhejnaa*

main मुख्य *mukhya;* **~ street** मुख्य सड़क *mukhya sadak*

make an appointment, to अपॉयंटमेंट लेना *appointment lena*

make-up श्रृंगार *shringaar*

male पुरुष *purush*

mallet लकड़ी का हथौड़ा *lakdee kaa hathodaa*

man पुरुष *purush*

manager प्रबंधक *prabundhuk*

manicure मैनीक्योर *manicure*

manual [car] मेन्युअल *manual*

map नक्शा *naksha*

March मार्च *march*

margarine कृत्रिम मक्खन *kritrim makhan*

market बाज़ार *bazaar*

married, to be शादीशुदा होना *shaadi shudaa hona*

mascara मैसकारा *mascara*

mask [diving] नकाब *nakaab*

mass सभा *sabha*

massage मालिश *maalish*

match (soccer, etc.) मैच *match*

matches मैचों *matchon*

matinée अपराह्न का शो *apraahan*

matter: it doesn't matter विषय: यह मायने नहीं रखता *vishay: yeh maayne nahin rakhta*

what's the matter? क्या बात है? *kya baat hai*

mattress गद्दा *gudda*

May मई *mai*

may I ? क्या मैं? *kya main*

maybe शायद *shaayad*

me मुझे *mujhe*

mean, to मतलब *mutlub*

measles खसरा *khusraa*

measure, to मापना *maapnaa*

measurement माप *map*

meat मांस *maans*

medical certificate मेडीकल प्रमाणपत्र *medical pramanpatra*

medication इलाज *ilaaj*

medium मध्यम *madhyam*

meet, to मिलना *milnaa* **pleased to meet you** आप से मिल कर खुशी हुई *aap se mil kur khushi hui*

meeting place [point] मिलने की जगह *milne kee jagah*

member सदस्य *sadasya*

men (toilets) पुरुष *purush*

mention: don't mention it चर्चा: कृपया चर्चा ना करें *churcha: kripyaa churchaa naa Karen*

menu मेनू *menu*

message संदेश *sandesh*

metal धातु *dhaatu*

meter (in taxi) मीटर *meter*

metro मेट्रो *metro;* **\~ station** मेट्रो स्टेशन *metro station*

microwave माइक्रोवेव *microwave*

midday मध्याह्न *madhyah*

midnight मध्यरात्रि *madhyaratree*

migraine माइग्रेन *migraine*

mileage माइलेज *mileage*

milk दूध *dhoodh;* **with** \~ दूध के साथ *dhoodh ke saath*

million दस लाख *das lakh*

mind: do you mind if ...? बुरा मानना: आपको बुरा तो नहीं लगेगा अगर ... ? *bura manna: aapko bura to nahin lagega agur...*

mine मेरा *mera;* **it's mine!** यह मेरा है! *yeh mera hai*

mineral water मिनरल वाटर *mineral water*

mini-bar मिनी-बार *mini-bar*

minimart मिनी-मार्ट *mini-mart*

minute मिनट *minute*

mirror आईना *ainaa*

missing, to be खो जाना
kho jaana

mistake गलती *galtee*

mobile home चलनशील
घर *chalansheel ghar*

modern आधुनिक
aadhunik

moisturizer
मॉश्चराइजर *moistur-izer*

monastery मठ *muth*

Monday सोमवार *somvaar*

money धन *dhun*; ~
order मनी ऑर्डर
money order

month महीना *mahinaa*;

monthly मासिक *maasik*

moped मोपेड *moped*

more और *aur*; **I'd like
some more** ... मुझे
कुछ और ... चाहिए
*mujhe kuch aur
chahiye...*

morning, in the सुबह में
subah mein

mosque मस्जिद *masjid*

mosquito bite मच्छर
का काटना उंबीबीत
ां जंद

mosquito मच्छर
machchhar

mosquito net मच्छ.
रदानी *machchhardani*

mother माँ *maa*

motion sickness गति
संबंधी बीमारी *gati
sambhundhee bimaaree*

motorbike मोटरबाइक
motorbike

motorboat मोटरबोट
motorboat

motorway मोटरवे
motorway

mountain पर्वत *parvat*;
~ **bike** पर्वतीय साइ.

किल *parvatiye cycle*;
~ **pass** पर्वतीय रास्ता
parvatiye raasta; ~
range पर्वतीय श्रृंखला
parvatiye shrinkhala

moustache मूँछ *mooch*

mouth मुँह *moonh*; ~
ulcer मुँह का अल्सर
moonh kaa ulcer

move, to हिलना *hilnaa*;
don't move him!
उसे मत हिलाओ! *use
mut hilao*

movie सिनेमा *cinema*;
~ **theater** सिनेमा
थियेटर *cinema theater*

Mr. श्रीमान् *shrimaan*

Mrs. श्रीमती *shrimatee*

much ज्यादा *jyaada*

mugged, to be हमला
होना *humlaa hona*

mugging हमला *humlaa*

mugs मग *mug*

multiple journey बहु
यात्रा *bahu yaatra*

multiplex cinema
मल्टीप्लेक्स सिनेमा
multiplex cinema

mumps मम्प्स *mumps*

muscle मॉंसपेशी
maanspeshi

museum संग्रहालय
sanghralaya

music संगीत *sangeet*

musician संगीतकार
sangeetkaar

must: I must होना: मुझे
... चाहिए *hona: mujhe
...chahiye*

mustard सरसों *sarson*

my मेरा *mera*

myself: I'll do it myself
स्वयं: मैं यह स्वयं
करूंगा *wain: main yeh
swain karoongaa*

N

name नाम *naam*; **my
name is** मेरा नाम है
mera naam hai; **what's
your name?** आपका
नाम क्या है? *aapkaa
naam kya hai*; **what's
your surname?**
आपका उपनाम क्या
है? *aapkaa upnaam
kya hai*

napkin नैपकीन *napkin*

nappies नैपिज
nappies

narrow संकरा *sunkraa*

national राष्ट्रीय
rashtriya

nationality राष्ट्रीयता
rashtriyeetaa

nature reserve
प्राकृतिक संपदा
prakritik sampadaa

nausea जी मचलाहट
jee muchlaahut

near निकट *nikut*
~**sighted** निकट दृष्टि
nikut drishtee

nearest निकटतम
nikuttum

nearby आसपास
aaspaas

necessary आवश्यक
aavshayak

neck गर्दन *gurdan*

necklace माला *maala*

nephew भतीजा/भांजा
bhatijaa/bhaanjaa

nerve नस *nus*

nervous system
नाड़ी-मंडल *naadi-mundal*

never कभी नहीं *kabhi
nahin*; ~ **mind** बुरा ना
मानें *bura naa maane*

new नया *naya*

New Year नया साल
naya saal

New Zealand न्यूजीलैंड
new zealand

New Zealander
न्यूजीलैंड वासी *new
zealand vaasi*

newspaper समाचार पत्र
samachar patra

**newsstand [newsa-
gent]** समाचारपत्र की
दुकान *samachaar patra
kee dukaan*

next अगला *aglaa*

next to... के बाद ... *ke
baad...*

next stop! अगला स्टॉप
aglaa stop

nice अच्छा *acha*

niece भतीजी/भांजी
bhatijee/bhaanjee

night: at ~ रात: रात में
raat: raat mein; ~**club**
नाइट क्लब *night club*

no नहीं *nahin*

no one कोई नहीं *koi
nahin*

no way! हरगिज़ नहीं!
hargeej nahin

noisy कोलाहलपूर्ण
kolahulpurn

non-alcoholic अल.
कोहल रहित *alcohol
rahit*

non-smoking गैर- ६
.्रूमपान *gair dhrumpaan*

none एक भी नहीं *ek
bhi nahin*

nonsense! बकवास!
bukwaas

noon मध्यान्ह *mudhyaan*

normal सामान्य
saamaanyaa

north उत्तर *uttar*

nose नाक *naak*

not: not bad नहीं: बुरा नहीं *nahin: bura nahin*

not good अच्छा नहीं *acha nahin*

not yet अभी तक नहीं *abhi tuk nahin*

note संकेत *sanket*

nothing else और कुछ नहीं *aur kuch nahin*

notify, to सूचना देना *soochnaa dena*

November नवंबर *navambar*

now अब *ab*

numbers संख्या *sankhyaa*

number plate नंबर प्लेट *number plate*

nurse देखभाल *dekhbaal*

nylon नाइलोन *nylon*

O

o'clock: it's ... o'clock बजे: अभी ... बजा है *baje: abhi ... baja hai*

occasionally कभी-कभी *kabhi-kabhi*

occupied व्यस्त *vyast*

October अक्तूबर *uctoober*

odds lEeHkkouk *sambhaavnaa*

of course बिल्कुल *bilkul*

off licence गैर लाइसेंसी *gair licensee*

off-peak सामान्य काल *samanya kaal*

office कार्यालय *karayalaya*

often अक्सर *aksar*

oil तेल *tel*

okay ठीक *theek*

old पुराना *puraanaa* ~ **town** पुराना शहर *puraana sheher;*

~-fashioned पुराने फैशन का *puraane fashion kaa*

olive oil जैतून का तेल *jaitoon kaa tel*

omelet ऑमलेट *omelet*

on में *mein; ~* **foot** पैदल *paidal; ~* **my own** अपने बलबूते *apne balbutte; ~* **the hour** समय पर *samy pur; ~* **the left** बाएं की ओर *bayan ki aur; ~* **the other side** दूसरी दिशा में *doosree dishaa mein; ~* **the right** दाहिने की ओर *dahine kee aur; ~* **the spot** स्थल पर *sthal pur*

on/off switch चालू/बंद चरम *chaalu/bund switch*

once एकबार *ek baar*

one: ~-way एक: एकतरफा *ek: ektarfaa; ~-way* **street** एकतरफा सड़क *ektarfaa sadak; ~-way* **ticket** एकतरफा टिकट *ektarfaa ticket; ~* **like that** उस तरह का *us tarah kaa*

open खुला *khulla,* **open, to** खोलना *kholnaa*

opening hours खुले रहने का समय *khule rehne kaa samay*

opera संगीत नाटक *sangeet natak; ~* **house** संगीत नाट्यशाला *sangeet natayashaala*

operation शल्य चिकित्सा *shulya chikitsaa*

opposite विरुद्ध *veerudh*

optician ऑप्टिशियन *optician*

or या *yaa*

orange संतरा *santraa*

orchestra आर्केस्ट्रा *orchestra*

order, to ऑर्डर करना *order karnaa*

organized hike/walk संगठित सैर/पैदल चालन *sangatith sair/ paidal chulnaa*

our(s) हमारा *hamaraa*

outdoor आउटडोर *outdoor*

outrageous निर्लज्ज *nirluj*

outside बाहर *baahar*

oval अंडाकार *undakaar*

oven चूल्हा *chulhaa*

over there वहाँ पर *wahan pur*

overcharge: I've been overcharged अधिक मूल्य लेना: मुझ से अधिक मूल्य ले लिया गया है *adhik mulya lena: mujh se adhik mulya le liya gaya hai*

overdone अधिक पका *adhik paka*

overheat अधिक गर्म *adhik garam*

overnight रात भर में *raat bahr mein*

owe, to ऋणी होना *rinee hona;* **how much do I owe?** मुझे कितना देना है? *mujhe kitna dena hai*

own: on my own अपना: अपने बलबूते *apna: apne bulbute*

owner स्वामी *swami*

P

p.m. अपराहन *apraahan*

pacifier शांत करने वाला *shaant karne waala*

pack, to भरना *bhurnaa*

package पुलिन्दा *pulindaa*

packed lunch बंद दोपहर का भोजन *bund dopaher kaa bhojan*

packet of cigarettes सिगरेट का डब्बा *cigarette ka dubba*

padlock ताला *taala*

pail बाल्टी *baaltee*

pain: to be in दर्द: दर्द में होना *dard: dard mein hona; ~* **killers** दर्दनाशक *dardnaashak*

paint, to चित्रकारी करना *chitrakaari karnaa*

painter चित्रकार *chitrakar*

painting चित्रकला *chitrkalaa*

pair of, a एक जोड़ी *ek jodi*

palace महल *mahal*

palpitations धड़कन *dhadkan*

panorama चित्रावली *chitravali*

pants पैंट *pant*

pantyhose पैंटीहोज़ *pantyhose*

paper कागज़ *kagaaj; ~* **napkins** कागजी नैपकीन *kaagzee napkin*

paracetamol पैरासी. टामोल *paracetamol*

paraffin पैराफिन *paraffin*

paralysis लकवा *lukwaa*

parcel पार्सल *parcel*
pardon? माफ़ी? *maafi*
parents माता-पिता
mata-pita
park पार्क *park*
park, to पार्क करना
park kurnaa
parking lot पार्किंग
parking
parking meter पार्किंग
मीटर *parking meter*
parliament building
संसद भवन *sansad
bhawan*
**partner (boyfriend/
girlfriend)**
सहयोगी *sahyogi*
parts पुर्ज़ा *purjaa*
party पार्टी *party*
pass, to गुज़रना
gujurnaa
pass through, to से
गुज़रना *se gujurnaa*
passport पासपोर्ट
passport
pastry store पेस्ट्री
की दुकान *pastry kee
dukaan*
patch, to पैबंद लगाना
paibund lagaana
patient (*n.*) धैर्यवान
dhairyawaan
pavement, on the फ़र्श
पर *phursh pur*
pay, to भुगतान करना
bhugtaan karnaa ~
a fine जुर्माना देना
jurmaana dena
pay phone पे फ़ोन *pe
phone*
payment भुगतान
bhugtaan
peak शीर्ष *shirsh*
pearl मोती *moti*
pedestrian: ~ crossing

पैदल चलने वाला:
पैदल चलने वालों के
लिए क्रॉसिंग *paidal
chalne waala: paidal
chalne waalon ke liye
crossing;* **~ zone** पैदल
चलने वालों का क्षेत्र
*paidal chalne waalon
ka shetre*
pen कलम *kalam*
pencil पेंसिल *pencil*
penknife कलम बनाने
का चाकू *kalam banene
kaa chaaku*
people लोग *log*
pepper काली मिर्च *kaali
mirch*
per: ~ day प्रति: प्रतिदिन
prati : pratidin; **~ hour**
प्रति घंटा *prati ghuntaa;*
~ night प्रति रात्रि
orati ratree; **~ week**
प्रति सप्ताह *prati
saptaah*
perhaps शायद *shaayad*
period (menstrual)
माहवारी *maahwaari* **~
pains** माहवारी का दर्द
maahwaari ka dard
perm, to बाल घुंघराले
कराना *baal ghungraale
karnaa*
petrol पेट्रोल *petrol;* **~
station** पेट्रोल स्टेशन
petrol station
pewter काँसा *kaansaa*
pharmacy दवाख़ाना
dawakhaana
phone: ~card फ़ोन:
फ़ोन कार्ड *phone:
phone card;* **~ call**
फ़ोन कॉल *phone call*
phone, to फ़ोन करना
phone karma
photo: to take ~ चित्र:

चित्र लेना *chitra:
chitra lena*
passport-size
पासपोर्ट-आकार चित्र
paassport-aakaar chitra
photocopier
फोटोकोपियर
photocopier
photographer
फोटोग्राफ़र *photog-
rapher*
phrase वाक्यखंड
vaakyakhund
phrase book वाक्यखंड
की पुस्तक *vaakyak-
hund kee pustak*
pick someone up, to
किसी को लेना *kisi
ko lena*
pick up, to किसी को
लेना *kisi ko lena*
picnic पिकनिक *picnic;*
~ area पिकनिक क्षेत्र
picnic shetre
piece हिस्सा *hissa; a
piece of* एक हिस्सा
का *ek hissa ka;*
pill गोली *goli*
**Pill (contraceptive): to
be on the Pill** गोली:
गोली के सहारे रहना
*goli: goli ke sahare
rehnaa*
pillow तकिया *tukiyaa;* **~
case** तकिया का खोल
tukiyaa kaa khol
pilot light पायलट लाइट
pilot light
pink गुलाबी *gulaabi*
pipe (smoking) पाइप
pipe
pitch (for camping) टेंट
लगाना *tent lagaana*
pizzeria पिज़्ज़ेरीया
pizzeria

place (*n.*) जगह *jagah*
place a bet, to दांव
लगाना *daanv laganaa*
plane जहाज *jahaj*
plans कल्पना *kalpanaa*
plant (*n.*) पौधा *paudha*
plastic: ~ bags
प्लास्टिक: प्लास्टिक
बैग *plastic: plastic
bag;* **~ wrap** प्लास्टिक
का आवरण *plastic kaa
aavran*
plate थाली *thaali*
platform प्लेटफॉर्म
platform
platinum प्लेटिनम
platinum
play, to (music) बजाना
bajana **~ group** खेल
समूह *khel samooh;* **~
ground** खेल का मैदान
khel kaa maidaan
playing field खेल
का मैदान *khel kaa
maidaan*
playwright नाटककार
natakkaar
pleasant सुहाना
suhaana
please कृपया *kripyaa*
plug प्लग *plug*
p.m. अपराहन *apraahun*
pneumonia निमोनिया
pneumonia
point of interest
आकर्षण बिंदु *aakarshun
bindu*
point to to, to को दिखाना
ko dikhaana
poison ज़हर *zaher*
police पुलिस *police;* **~
report** पुलिस रिपोर्ट
police report; **~ station**
पुलिस स्टेशन *police
station*

pollen count पराग गणना *parag gunnaa*

polyester पोलीस्टर *polyester*

pond तालाब *talaab*

pop (music) पॉप *pop*

popcorn पॉप कॉर्न *pop corn*

popular प्रसिद्ध *praseedh*

port बंदरगाह *bandurgaah*

porter (hotel) पोर्टर *porter* (train station) कुली *kulee*

portion जगह *jagah*

possible: as soon as possible संभव: जितनी जल्दी संभव हो सके *sambhuv: jitnaa jaldee sambhuv ho sake*

possibly संभवत *sambhuvate*

post (mail) डाक *daak* ~ **office** डाकघर *daakghar;* ~ **box** पोस्ट बॉक्स *post box;* ~ **card** पोस्ट कार्ड *post card*

post, to डाक भेजना *daak bhejnaa*

postage डाक खर्च *daak khurch*

potato chips आलू चिप्स *aaloo chips*

potatoes आलू *aaloo*

pottery कुम्हारी विद्या *kumhaari vidya*

pound (sterling) पाउंड *pound*

power: ~ **cut** बिजली: बिजली कटौती *bijlee: bijlee katautee;* ~ **points** बिजली के प्वाइंट *bijlee ke point*

pregnant, to be गर्भवती होना *garbhvati hona*

premium (gas/petrol) प्रीमियम *premium*

prescribe, to व्यवस्था करना *vyavusthaa karnaa*

prescription निर्देश *nirdesh*

present (gift) उपहार *uphaar*

press, to दबाना *dabanaa*

pretty सुंदर *sundur*

priest पुजारी *pujaari*

prison कारागार *karagaar*

probably शायद *shaayad*

produce store [grocer] किराने थ्क दुकान *kiraane kee dukaan*

program कार्यक्रम *karayakaram;* ~ **of events** कार्यक्रम की सूची *karayakaram kee soochi*

pronounce, to निर्णय सुनाना *nirnay sunnaa*

pub पब *pub*

public building सार्वजनिक भवन *saarvajanik bhawan*

pump पंप *pump*

puncture पंचर *puncture*

puppet show कठपुतली का खेल *kuthputlee kaa khel*

pure: pure cotton शुद्ध: शुद्ध सूती *shudh: shudh sooti*

purple बैंगनी *bainganee*

purse पर्स *purse*

put: where can I put? रखना: मैं कहाँ रख सकता हूँ? *rukhnaa: main kahan rukh saktaa hoon*

quality गुणवत्ता *gunvutta*

quantity मात्रा *maatraa*

quarter चौथाई *chauthai;* ~ **past** बनकर पंद्रह मिनट *bujkur pandrah minute;* ~ **to** बजने में पंद्रह मिनट *bajne mein pandrah minute*

queue, to पंक्ति में खड़े होना *panktee mein khade hona*

quick तेज *tej*

quickest: what's the quickest way? सबसे तेज: सबसे तेज तरीका क्या है? *sabse tej: sabse tarikaa kya hai*

quickly तेजी से *teji se*

quiet शांत *shaant*

quieter अधिक शांति *adhik shaantee*

race track [racecourse] रेसकोर्स *race course*

racket रैकेट *racket*

railway रेल *rail*

rain, to बारिश होना *bearish hona*

raincoat बरसाती *barsaatee*

rape बलात्कार *balatkaar*

rapids झरना *jhurnaa*

rare अतुल्य *atulyaa*

rash चकता *chuktaa*

rather प्राय *prayah*

razor रेजर *razoti;* ~ **blades** रेजर ब्लेड *razor blade*

reading पढ़ना *padhnaa*

ready तैयार *tayyaar*

real वास्तविक *vastaavik*

really? सचमुच? *suchmuch*

receipt रसीद *raseed*

reception (desk) स्वागत *swagat*

receptionist रिसेप्शनिस्ट *receptionist*

recommend, to सलाह देना *salaah dena;* **can you recommend?** क्या आप सलाह दे सकते हैं? *kya aap salaah de sakte hain;* **what do you recommend?** आप क्या सलाह दे सकते हैं? *aap kya salaah de sakte hain*

red लाल *laal;* ~ **wine** रेड वइन *red wine*

reduction कमी *kami*

refreshments जलपान *jalpaan*

refrigerator रेफ्रिजरेटर *refrigerator*

refund वापसी *waapsi*

regards: give my regards to आदर: को मेरा आदर देना *aadur ko mera aadur dena*

region क्षेत्र *shetre*

registered mail पंजीकृत मेल *panjeekrit mail*

registration form पंजीकरण फॉर्म *panjeekaran form*

registration number (car) पंजीकरण संख्या *panjeekaran sankhya*

regular नियमित *niyamit*

religion धर्म *dharma*

remember: I don't remember याद करना: मुझे याद नहीं *yaad kurnaa: mujhe yaad nahin*

rent, to ~ out किराया, किराए पर देना *kiraaya, kiraaye pur dena;*
I'd like to rent मैं किराए पर लेना चाहुंगा *main kiraay pur lena chahoongaa*

repair, to मरम्मत करना *murummut karnaa*

repairs मरम्मत *murummut*

repeat, to दोहराना *dorahnaa;* **please repeat that** कृपया उसे दोहराएं *kripyaa use dohraaye*

replacement बदल *badal;* **~ part** बदला हुआ पुर्जा *badlaa hua purjaa*

report, to बताना *bataanaa*

require, to आकांक्षा करना *aakaanshaa karnaa*

required, to be आकांक्षा होना *aakaanshaa hona*

reservation आरक्षण *aarakshun*

reservations desk आरक्षण डेस्क *aaruks-hun desk*

reserve, to आरक्षण करना *aarukshun kurnaa;* **I'd like to reserve** मैं आरिक्षत करना चाहुंगा *main aarakshit karnaa chahoongaa*

rest, to आराम करना *aaraam kurnaa*

restaurant रेस्टोरेंट *restaurant*

retail खुदरा *khudra*

retired, to be अवकाश

return *(adj.)* वापसी *waapsee;* **~ ticket** वापसी टिकट *waapsee ticket*

return, to वापस होना *waapus hona*

reverse the charges, to शुल्क उल्टा कर देना *shulk ulta kur dena*

revolting राजद्रोही *raajdrohi*

rheumatism गठिया *guthiyaa*

rib पसली *puslee*

rice चावल *chaawal*

right *(direction)* **: on the ~** दाएं: दाहिने की ओर *daanyan: daahine kee aur*

right *(correct)* ठीक *theek;* **that's ~** यह ठीक है *yeh theek hai*

right of way रास्ते पर अधिकार *raaste pur adhikaar*

ring अंगूठी *angoothi*

rip-off *(n.)* डकैती *dacaitee*

river नदी *nadi;* **~ cruise** नदी क्रूज़ *nadi cruise*

road सड़क *sadak;* **~ map** सड़क मानचित्र *sadak maanchitra;* **~ closed** सड़क बंद *sadak bund*

robbed, to be लूट लिया जाना *loot liya jaana*

robbery डकैती *dacaitee*

rock music रॉक संगीत *rock sangeet*

rolls रौल्स *rolls*

romantic रोमांटिक *romantic*

roof छत *chhut* **~-rack** रूफ रैक *roof rack*

room कमरा *kumara;* **~ service** रूम सेवा *room seva*

rope रस्सी *rassi*

round गोलाई *golaai~* **neck** गोल गला *gol gala*

round *(of golf)* राउंड *round*

round-trip वापसी *waap-see* **~ ticket** वापसी का टिकट *waapsee kaa ticket*

route मार्ग *marg*

rubbish कूड़ा-करकट *kooda-kurkut*

rude, to be असभ्य होना *asabhya hona*

ruins खंडहर *khundhur*

run: ~ into भिड़ंत *bhidant* **~ out** समाप्त होना *samapt hona*

running shoes दौड़ने वाला जूता *daudne waala jota*

rush hour भीड़ वाला समय *bheed waala samay*

S

safari सफारी *safari*

safari park सफारी पार्क *safari park*

safe *(n.)* फ्रिकज्श *tijoree*

safe *(adj.)* सुरक्षित *surukshit* **to feel ~** सुरक्षित महसूस करना *surukshit mehsoos karnaa*

safety सुरक्षा *surukshaa;* **~ pins** सेफ्टी पिन *safety pin*

salad सलाद *salad*

sales बिक्री *bikree;* **~ tax** बिक्री कर *bikree kar*

salt नमक *namak*

salty नमकीन *namkeen*

same समान *samaan*

sand रेत *rait*

sandals सैंडल *sandal*

sandwich सैंडविच *sandwich*

sandy रेतीला *raiteela*

sanitary napkins [towels] तौलिया *tauliyaa*

satellite TV सेटेलाइट टीवी *satellite TV*

satin साटन *satin*

satisfied: I'm not satisfied with this संतुष्ट: मैं इससे संतुष्ट नहीं हूँ *santusht: main isse santusht nahin hona*

Saturday शनिवार *shanivaar*

sauce चटनी *chutney*

saucepan सॉस पैन *saucepan*

sauna सौना *sauna*

sausages सॉसेज़ *sausages*

say: how do you say? कहना: आप कैसे कहते हैं? *kehna: aap kaise kehte hain*

scan *(computer)* स्कैन ;कंप्यूटरद्ध *scan (computer)*

scarf दुपट्टा *dupatta*

scenic route दर्शनीय रास्ता *darshniye raasta*

scheduled flight पूर्वनिर्धारित उड़ान *purvnidhaarit udaan*

school विद्यालय *vidyalaya*

sciatica साइटिका

saitika

scissors कैंची *kainchi*

scooter स्कूटर *scooter*

screwdriver स्क्रू ड्राइवर *screwdriver*

sea समुद्र *samudra*

seafront सी-फ्रंट *sea-front*

seasick: I feel ~ मैं सी-सिकनेस: मैं सी-सिकनेस महसूस कर रहा हूँ *sea sickness: main sea sickness mehsoos kur raha hoon*

season ticket सीज़न टिकट *season ticket*

seasoning सीज़निंग *seasoning*

seat बैठने की जगह *baithne kee jagah*

is this seat taken? यह सीट भरी है? *kya yeh seat bhari hai*

second द्वितीय *dweetee-eye; ~ class (ticket)* द्वितीय श्रेणी (टिकट) *dweeteeye shreenee (ticket); ~-hand* पुराना *puraana*

secretary सचिव *sachiv*

sedative शांतिकर दिजपांत

see, to देखना *dekhnaa*

see you soon! फिर मिलते हैं! *phir milte hain*

self-employed, to be स्व-रोज़गार होना *swa-rozgaar hona*

self-service स्व-सेवा *swa-sewa*

send, to भेजना *bhejnaa*

senior citizen वरिष्ठ नागरिक *varisht naagrik*

---

separated, to be अलग होना *alag hona*

separately अलग अलग *lag alag*

September सितंबर *sitambar*

serious(ly) गंभीरताप.. वूक *gambhirtaapurvuk*

served, to be परोसना *parosnaa*

service सेवा *sewa*

is service included? क्या सेवा शुल्क शामिल है? *kya sewa shulk shaamil hai*

serviette सर्वीएट *serviette*

set menu मेनू सेट करें *menu set karen*

sex (act) सेक्स *sex*

shade (color) रंग *rang*

shady छायादार *chayaadaar*

shallow छिछला *chichlaa*

shampoo शैंपू ॉ उचववय *~ and set* शैंपू शैंपू सेट करवाना *shampoo aur set karnaa*

shape आकार *aakaar*

share, to हिस्सेदारी करना *hissedaari karma*

sharp items नुकीला सामान *nukeela samaan*

shaving: ~ brush शेविंग: शेविंग ब्रश *shaving: shaving brush; ~ cream* शेविंग क्रीम *shaving cream*

she यह *weh*

sheet (bedding) चादर *chaadur*

ship जहाज़ *jahaj*

shirt कमीज़ *kameez*

---

shock (electric) झटका *jhutka*

shoe repair जूता मरम्मत *jota murummut*

shoe store जूते की दुकान *joote kee dukaan*

shoes जूते *joote*

shop दुकान *dukaan; ~ assistant* दुकान में सहायक *dukaan mein sahayak*

shopping: ~ area खरीदारी: खरीदारी क्षेत्र *khareedaari: khareedaari shetre; ~ basket* खरीदारी वाली टोकरी *khareedaari waali tokree; ~mall [centre]* शॉपिंग मॉल *shopping mall~ trolley* शॉपिंग ट्रॉली *shopping trolley; to go ~* खरीदारी के लिए जाना *khareedaari ke liye jaana*

short छोटा *chotaa; ~-sighted* सूक्ष्म दृष्टि *suksham drishti*

shorts शॉर्ट्स *shorts*

shoulder *da/kk* कंधा *kandha*

shovel बेलचा *belcha*

show, to दिखाना *dikhaana*

shower शावर *shower*

shut बंद करना *bund karnaa;*

when do you shut? आप कब बंद करते हैं *aap kun bund karte hain*

sick: I'm going to be sick बीमार: मैं बीमार होने वाला हूँ *bimaar: main bimaar hone waala hoon*

side (of road) किनारा

किनारा *~ street* किनारे वाली गली *kinaare waali gali*

side order साइड ऑर्डर *side order*

sides (hair) बगलें *buglein*

sights दृश्य *drishya*

sightseeing: ~ tour दृश्यावलोकन: दृश्यावलोकन भ्रमण *drishyavlokan: drishyavlokan;*

to go ~ दृश्यावलोकन के लिए जाना *drishyaavlokan ke liye jaana*

sign संकेत *sanket*

signpost मार्ग-सूचक स्तंभ *marg-soochak stumbh*

silk रेशम *reshum*

silver चांदी *chaandi; ~-plate* चांदी की थ.. ली *chaandi kee thaili*

singer गायक *gaayak*

single एकल *ekal ~ room* सिंगल कमरा *single kamraa; ~ ticket* सिंगल टिकट *single ticket; to be ~* अविवाहित होना *avivaahit hona*

sink डूबना *doobnaa*

sister बहन *bahan*

sit, to बैठना *baithnaa*

sit down, बैठ जाओ *baith jao; please* कृपया *kripyaa*

size आकार *aakaar*

skin त्वचा *twacha*

skirt स्कर्ट *skirt*

sleep, to सोना *sona*

sleeping: ~ bag सोना: सोने वाला बैग *sona: sone waala bag;*

car शयनयान कार *shayanyaan car;* ~ **pill** नींद की गोली *neend kee goli*

sleeve बाजू *baaju*

slice टुकड़ा *tukdaa*

slippers चप्पल *chappal*

slow धीमा *dheema;* **to be** ~ धीमा चलना *dheema chulna*

slow down! धीमे हो जाओ! *dheeme ho jao*

slowly धीमे से *dheeme se*

small छोटा *chota;* ~ **change (coins)** छोटे खुल्ले *chote khulle*

smell: there's a bad smell गंध: कुछ बदबू है *gandh: kuch badboo hai*

smoke, to धूम्रपान करना *dhrumpaan karnaa*

smoking धूम्रपान *dhrumpaan*

snack bar स्नैक बार *snack bar*

snacks स्नैक *snack*

sneakers जूता *jota*

snorkel स्नोर्केल *snorkel*

snow, to बर्फ पड़ना *burf padnaa*

soap साबुन *saabun*

soap powder साबुन का पाउडर *saabun kaa powder*

soccer फुटबॉल *football*

socket सॉकेट *socket*

socks जुराबें *juraabe*

soft drink सॉफ्ट ड्रिंक *soft drink*

solarium सोलेरियम *solarium*

sole (shoes) सोल *sole*

soluble aspirin घुलनशील एस्प्रीन *ghulnashil aspirin*

some कुछ *kuch*

someone कोई *koi*

something कुछ *kuch*

sometimes कई बार *kai baar*

son बेटा *beta*

soon जल्दी *jaldee*

soon: as soon as possible जल्दी: जितनी जल्दी संभव हो सके *jaldee: jitni jaldee sambhav ho sake*

sore: it's ~ व्रण: व्रण है *vrana: vrana hai;* ~ **throat** कंठव्रण *kanthavrana*

sorry! क्षमा! *shama*

sort क्रम *krum*

soul music जीवन संगीत *jeevan sangeet*

sour खट्टा *khutta*

south दक्षिण *dakshin*

South Africa दक्षिण अफ्रीका *dakshin africa*

souvenir स्मारिका *smaarikaa;* ~ **store** स्मारिका की दुकान *smaarikaa kee dukaan*

soy sauce सोयाबीन की चटनी *soyabean kee chutney*

space स्थान *sthaan*

spare (extra) अतिरिक्त *atirikt*

speak, to बोलना *bolnaa;* ~ **to** से बोलना *se bolnaa;*

do you speak English? क्या आप अंग्रेजी बोलते हैं? *kya aap angreji bolte hain*

special: ~ **delivery** विशेष: विशेष वितरण *vishesh: vishesh vitrun;* ~ **rate** विशेष दर *vishesh dur*

specialist विशेषज्ञ *visheshyagya*

specimen नमूना *namoona*

speed, to गति बढ़ाना *gati badhnaa*

spend, to खर्च करना *khurch karnaa*

spicy मसालेदार *masaledaar*

sponge स्पंज *sponge*

spoon चम्मच *chummuch*

sport खेल *khel*

sporting goods store खेल के सामान की दुकान *khel ke samay kee dukaan*

sports खेल *khel;* ~ **club** स्पोर्ट्स क्लब *sports club;* ~ **ground** खेल का मैदान *khel kaa maidaan*

sprained, to be मोच आना *moch aana*

spring वसंत *vasant*

square चौकोर *chaukaur*

stadium स्टेडियम *stadium*

staff कर्मचारी *karamchaari*

stain धब्बा *dhubba*

stainless steel स्टेनलेस स्टील *stainless steel*

stairs सीढ़ियाँ *seedheeyaan*

stamp टिकट *ticket;* ~ **machine** टिकट की मशीन *ticket kee machine*

stand in line, to पंक्ति में खड़ा होना *punktee*

mein khadaa hona

standby ticket वैक. ल्पिक टिकट *vaikulpik ticket*

start, to आरंभ करना *aarambh karnaa*

statement (legal) वक्तव्य *vaktavya*

station स्टेशन *station*

statue मूर्ति *murtee*

stay (n.) पड़ाव *padaav*

stay, to ठहरना *thuharnaa*

steak house मांस खाने की जगह *maans khaane ki jagah*

sterilizing solution स्टेरिलाइजेशन सॉल्यूशन *sterilization solution*

stiff neck गर्दन में अकड़न *gardan mein akdun*

still: I'm still waiting अभी तक: मैं अभी तक इंतजार कर रहा हूं *abhi tuk: main abhi tuk intezaar kar raha hoon*

sting डंक *dunk*

stockings मोजा *mauza*

stolen, to be चुरा लिया गया *churaa liya hai*

stomach पेट *pet;* ~ **ache** पेट दर्द *pet dard*

stool मल *mul*

stop (bus) पड़ाव *padaav*

stop (at), to पर रुकना *pur ruknaa*

store दुकान *dukaan*

stormy, to be तूफानी होना *toofaani hona*

stove चूल्हा *chulhaa*

straight ahead सीधे सामने *seedhe saamne*

strained muscle मोच वाली मांसपेशी *mooch*

waali maanspeshi

strange अजीबोगरीब *ajeebogareeb*

straw *(drinking)* स्ट्रॉ *straw*

strawberry स्ट्रॉबेरी *strawberry*

stream धारा *dhaara*

strong शक्तिशाली *shakteeshaali*

student छात्र *chhatra*

study, to अध्ययन करना *adhyan kurnaa*

style शैली *shaili*

subtitled, to be सबटा. इटल्ड होना *subtitled hona*

subway मेट्रो *metro* ~ **station** मेट्रो स्टेशन *metro station*

sugar चीनी *cheenee*

suggest, to सुझाव देना *sujhaav dena*

suit उपयुक्त करना *upyukt karma*

suitable for उपयुक्त होना *upyukt hona*

summer गर्मी *garmi*

sun block सन ब्लॉक *sun block*

sunbathe, to धूप सेंकना *dhoop sainknaa*

sunburn सन बर्न *sun burn*

Sunday रविवार *ravivaar*

sunglasses धूप का चश्मा *dhoop ka chushma*

sunscreen सन-स्क्रीन *sun-screen*

sunshade सन शेड *sun shade*

sunstroke सूर्याघात *suryaghaat*

super *(gas/petrol)* सुपर *super*

superb उत्तम *uttam*

supermarket सुपरमाक.'ट *supermarket*

supervision पर्यवेक्षण *paryaveekshun*

supplement परिशिष्ट *parishisht*

suppositories सपोजिट्री *suppository*

sure: are you sure? विश्वस्त: क्या आप विश्वस्त हैं? *vishvust: kya aap vishvust hai*

surfboard सर्फ बोर्ड *surf board*

surname उपनाम *upnaam*

sweater स्वेटर *sweater*

sweatshirt स्वेट शॉर्ट *sweatshirt*

sweet मीठा *meetha*

sweets मिठाई *mithai*

swelling सूजन *soojun*

swim, to तैरना *tairnaa*

swimming तैराकी *tairaaki*; ~ **pool** स्वीमिंग पूल *swimming pool*; ~ **trunks** स्वीमिंग ट्रंक *swimming trunk*

swimsuit स्वीमिंग सूट *swimming suit*

switch स्विच *switch*

swollen, to be सूज जाना *sooch jaana*

symptoms लक्षण *lakshun*

synagogue यहूदियों का पूजा के लिए जमघट *yahoodiyon kaa pooja ke liye jumghut*

synthetic सिंथेटिक *synthetic*

T-shirt टी शर्ट *t-shirt*

table टेबल *table*

tablet टेबलेट *tablet*

take, to लेना *lena*

I'll take it मैं इसे लूंगा *main ise loonga*; ~ **out** निकलवाना *nikalwanaa* ~ **photographs, to** फोटो खींचना *photo kheenchnaa*

taken व्यस्त *vyast*

talk, to बात करना *baat kurnaa*

tall लंबा *lumba*

tampons टैम्पन *tampon*

tan त्वचा को धूप से भूरा करना *twacha ko dhoop se bhoora rakhna*

tap टोंटी *tontee*

taxi टैक्सी *taxi*; ~ **stand [rank]** टैक्सी स्टैंड *taxi stand*

tea चाय *chai*; ~ **bags** टी बैग *tea bag*; ~ **towel** टी टॉवेल *tea towel*

teacher शिक्षक *shikshak*

team टीम *team*

teaspoon चम्मच *chummuch*

teddy bear टेडी बियर *teddy bear*

telephone टेलीफोन *telephone*; ~ **booth** टेलीफोन बूथ *telephone booth*; ~ **call** टेलीफोन कॉल *telephone call*; ~ **directory** टेलीफोन डायरेक्ट्री *telephone directory*; ~ **number** टेलीफोन नंबर *telephone number*

telephone, to टेलीफोन करना *telephone kurnaa*

temperature तापमान *taapmaan*

temporarily अस्थाई रूप से *asthaai roop se*

ten thousand दस हजार *dus hazaar*

tennis टेनिस *tennis*; ~ **court** टेनिस कोर्ट *tennis court*

tent टेंट *tent*; ~ **pegs** टेंट खूँटी *tent khoontee*; ~ **pole** टेंट खंभा *tent khumbaa*

terrible भयंकर *bhayankar*

terrific शानदार *shaandaar*

tetanus टेटनिस *tetanus*

thali थाली *thali*

thank you धन्यवाद *dhanyawaad*

that one वह *weh*

that's all अब बस *ab bus*

theater नाट्यशाला *natyashaala*

theft चोरी *chori*

their(s) उनका *unka*

theme park थीम पार्क *theme park*

then तब *tub*

there वहां *wahan*

there is वहाँ है *wahan hai*

there are वहाँ हैं *wahan hai*

thermometer थर्मामीटर *thermometer*

thermos flask थर्मस फ्लास्क *thermos flask*

these ये *yeh*

they वे *weh*

thief चोर *chor*

thigh जांघ *jaangh*
thin पतला *putlaa*
think: ~ about it इस...
चबा: इस बारे में सोचें
*sochnaa: is bare mein
sochen;* **what do you
~ of ..?** आप ... के
बारे में क्या सोचते हैं?
*aap...ke bare mein kya
sochte hain*
I think *(feel)* मैं विचार
main vichaar
I think *(it seems)* मेरे
विचार से *mere
vichaar se*
third तृतीय *triteeye;*
~ party तृतीय पक्ष
triteeye paksh;
insurance बीमा *bema*,
third, एक तिहाई
ek tihai
thirsty: I am thirsty
प्यास: मैं प्यासा हूँ
pyaas: main pyaasa hoon
this यह *yeh;* **~ one**
यह *yeh*
those वे *weh*
thousand हजार *hazaar*
throat गला *gala*
thrombosis थ्रॉम्बोसिस
thrombosis
through द्वारा *dwaara*
thumb अंगूठा *angootha*
Thursday गुरुवार
guruvaar
ticket टिकट *ticket* **~
office** टिकट कार्यालय
ticket karayalaya
tie टाई *tie*
tiger बाघ *baagh*
tight तंग *tung*
tights टाइट्स *tights*
till receipt रसीद *raseed*
time समय *samay;* **on ~**
समय पर *samay pur;*

free ~ खाली समय
khaali samay; **... times
a day** ... बार
din mein ... **baar**
timetable समय-सारणी
samay-saarni
tin टिन *tin;* **~ opener**
टिन ओपनर *tin opener*
tire टायर (कार) *tire
(car)*
tired: I'm tired थकान:
मैं थका हूँ *thakaan:
main thakaa hoon*
tissues टिश्यू *tissue*
to तक *tuk*
tobacco तम्बाकू
tumbakoo
tobacconist तम्बाकू की
दुकान *tumbakoo kee
dukaan*
today आज *aaj*
toe पंजा *punja*
tofu सोयाबीन का पनीर
soyabean ka paneer
together साथ साथ
saath saath
toilet शौचालय *shauchalaya;* **~ paper** टॉयलेट
पेपर *toilet paper*
tomorrow कल *kul*
tongue जीभ *jheebh*
tonight आज रात
aaj raat
tonsilitis टांसिलाइटिस
tonsillitis
tonsils टांसिल *tonsil*
too भी *bhi;* **~ much**
बहुत ज्यादा *bahut
zyaadaa*
tooth दांत *daant;* **~
brush** टूथ ब्रश *tooth
brush;* **~ache** दांत का
दर्द *daant kaa dard;* **~
paste** टूथ पेस्ट *tooth
paste*

top शीर्ष *shirsh*
torch टॉर्च *torch*
torn: this is torn फट
जाना: यह फट गया
है *phut jaana: yeh phut
gaya hai*
tough कड़ा *kada*
tour भ्रमण *bhraman;*
~ guide भ्रमण गाइड
bhraman guide; **~ op-
erator** भ्रमण संचालक
brahman sanchaluk
tourist सैलानी *sailaani*
tow truck खींचने वाला
ट्रक *kheenchne waala
truck*
towards की दिशा में *kee
disha mein*
towel तौलिया *tauliya*
tower मीनार *minaar*
town शहर *sheher* **~ hall**
टाउन हॉल *town hall*
toy खिलौना *khilonaa;*
~ store खिलौनों की
दुकान *khilonon kee
dukaan*
traditional परंपरागत
paramparagat
traffic यातायात *yat-
ayaat;* **~ jam** यातायात
जाम *yatayaat jam;*
trail सामान्य पथ
saamanya path
trailer ट्रेलर *trailer*
train ट्रेन *train;* **~
station** ट्रेन स्टेशन
train station
training shoes प्रशिक्षण
के लिए जूते *prakshis-
hun ke liye joote*
tram ट्राम *tram*
transfer स्थानांतरण
sthanataran
transit, in संक्रमण में
sankraman mein

translate, to अनुवाद
करें *anuvaad karen*
translation अनुवाद
anuvaad
translator अनुवादक
anuvaaduuk
trash कूड़ा *kooda;* **~
cans** कूड़ा का डब्बा
kooda kaa dubba
travel: ~ agency
पर्यटक: ट्रेवल एजेंसी
paryatun: travel agency;
~ sickness यात्रा
संबंधित बीमारी *yatraa
sambundhit bimaai*
**traveler's check
[cheque]** ट्रेवलर चेक
traveler check
tray ट्रे *tray*
tree पेड़ *per*
trim ट्रिम करवाना *trim
kurwanaa*
trip यात्रा *yatraa*
have a good trip
आपकी यात्रा सुखद हो
aapki yaatra sukhud ho
trolley ट्रॉली *trolley*
trousers पतलून *putloon*
truck ट्रक *truk*
true: that's ~ सच:
वह सच है *such: weh
such hai*
that's not ~ वह सच नहीं
है *weh such nahin hai*
try on, to पहनकर करें
puryatun karen
Tuesday मंगलवार
mangalwaar
tumor ट्यूमर *tumor*
tunnel सुरंग *surung*
turn, to मुड़ना *moodh-
naa;* **~ down** कम
करें *kum karen* **~ off**
बंद करें *bund karen;* **~
on** चालू करें *chaaloo*

karen; **~ up** अधिक करें *adhik aren*

turning मुड़ना *moodhna*

TV टी वी *TV*

tweezers ट्वीज़र *tweezer*

twice दोबारा *dobaara*

twin bed ट्विन बेड *twin bed*

twist: I've twisted my ankle ऐंठन; मेरे पैर में ऐंठन हो गई है *ainthun: mere paer mein ainthun ho gayi hai*

two-door car दो दरवाज़े वाली कार *do durwaaje waali car*

type प्रकार *prakaar*

what type? किस प्रकार? *kis prakaar*

typical आदर्शभूत *adurshbhoot*

tyre टायर *tyre*

U

ugly बदसूरत *badsoorat*

ulcer नासूर *naasoor*

umbrella छाता *chaataa*

uncle चाचा *chacha*

unconscious, to be बेहोश होना *behosh hona*

under उभस *uhps neeche*

underdone अधपका *adhpaka*

underpants अंतर्वस्त्र *anturvastra*

underpass भूमिगत पारपथ *bhoomigut paarpath*

understand, to समझना *samjhnaa*

do you understand? क्या तुम समझे? *kya tum samjhe*

I don't understand मैं समझा नहीं। *main samjha nahin*

undress, to कपड़े उतारना *kapde uttarnaa*

uneven असमतल *asamtul*

unfortunately दुर्भाग्यवश *durbhayavush*

uniform यूनिफॉर्म *uniform*

unit इकाई *ikaai*

United States अमेरिका *america*

unlimited mileage माइलेज *mileage*

unlock, to खोलना *kholnaa*

unpleasant अप्रिय *apriye*

unscrew, to खोलना *kholnaa*

until तब तक *tub tuk*

up to तक तक *tuk*

upset stomach पेट खराब चमज तीतंड़ *upstairs* ऊपरी मंजिल *upree manzil*

urine पेशाब *peshaab*

use, to इस्तेमाल करना *istemaal karnaa*

use: for my personal use इस्तेमाल: मेरे निजी इस्तेमाल के लिए *istemaal: mere niji istemaal ke liye*

V

V-neck वी-गला *V-gala*

vacant खाली *khaali*

vacation, on छुट्टी पर *chutti pur*

vaccinated against, to be का टीका लगाना *ka tikka lagana*

vaginal infection योनि का संक्रमण *yoni kaa sankramun*

valet service वैले सेवा *valet sewa*

valid मान्य *manya*

validate, to प्रमाणित करना *pramanit kurnaa*

valley घाटी *ghaati*

valuable मूल्यवान *mulyavaan*

value मूल्य *mulya*

valve वॉल्व *valve*

vanilla वनिला *vanilla*

VAT वैट *VAT;* **~ receipt** वैट रसीद *VAT raseed*

vegan, to be शाकाहारी होना *shakahaari hona*

vegetables सब्जियां *subjiyan*

vegetarian शाकाहारी *shaakahaari*

to be शाकाहारी होना *shaakahari hona*

vehicle registration document वाहन रजिस्ट्रेशन कागजात *waahan registration kagzaat*

vein नस *nus*

venereal disease यौन रोग *yon rog*

ventilator रोशनदार *roshundaan*

very बहुत *bahut*

video: ~ game वीडियो: वीडियो खेल *video: video khel;* **~ recorder** वीडियो रिकॉर्डर *video recorder*

view: with a view of the sea दृश्य: समुद्र का दृश्य के साथ *drishya: samudra kaa drishya ke saath*

viewpoint दृश्यावलोकन स्थल *drishyavalokun sthul*

village गांव *gaon*

vinaigrette विनाएग्रेट *vinaigrette*

vineyard/winery अंगूर का बगीचा/वाइनरी *angoor ka bagichaa*

visa वीसा *visa*

visit आगमन *aagmun*

visit, to [v.] मिलना *milnaa*

visiting hours दर्शन करने का समय *darshan karne kaa samay*

vitamin tablets विटा. मिन टेबलेट *vitamin tablet*

volleyball वॉलीबॉल *volleyball*

voltage वॉल्टेज *voltage*

vomit, to उल्टी करना *ultee kurnaa*

W

wait (for), to प्रतीक्षा करना *prateeksha kurna*

wait! रुको! *ruko*

waiter वेटर *waiter*

waiting room प्रतीक्षालय *prateekshaalaya*

waitress वेट्रेस *waitress*

wake, to जगाना *jaganaa*

wake-up call वेक-अप कॉल *wake-up call*

walk [n.] पैदलचालन *paidulchaalun;* **walking route** पैदल चालन रास्ता *paidal chaalan raastaa*

wallet बटुआ *batuaa*

war memorial युद्ध रमृ. ारक *yudh samaaruk*

ward (hospital) वार्ड *ward*

warm गर्म *garam*

washbasin वोश बेसिन *washbasin*

washing: ~ machine वॉशिंग मशीन *washing: washing machine;* **~ powder** वॉशिंग पाउडर *washing powder*

washing-up liquid ध गुलाई वाला द्रव *dhulaai wala drava*

wasp बरें *burre*

watch ध्यान देना *dhyaan dena*

water पानी *paani;* **~ bottle** पानी की बोतल *paani kee bottle;* **~ heater** पानी गर्म करने वाला *paani garam karne waala;* **~ skis** वाटर स्की *water ski*

waterfall जलप्रपात *julprapaat*

waterproof वाटरप्रूफ *waterproof;* **~ jacket** वाटर-प्रूफ जैकेट *water-proof jacket*

wave लहर *laher*

waxing वेक्सिंग *waxing*

way तरफ *taraf*

on the की तरफ *kee taraf*

we हमलोग *humlog*

wear, to पहनना *pehennaa*

weather मौसम

mausam; **~ forecast** मौसम पूर्वानुमान *mausam purvaaun*

wedding शादी *shaadi;* **~ ring** शादी की अंगूठी *shaadi kee angoothi*

Wednesday बुधवार *budhwaar*

week सप्ताह *week*

weekend: on [at] the ~ साप्ताहांत: सप्ता. हांत पर *saptaahaant: saptaahaant pur;* **~ rate** साप्ताहांत दर *saptaahaant dur*

weight: my weight is वजन: मेरा वजन है *vajan: mera vajan hai*

welcome to में स्वागत है *mein swaagat hai*

well-done (meat) बहुत अच्छा *bahut achaa*

west पश्चिमी *paschimi*

wetsuit वेट सूट *wet suit*

what: what time? क्या: कितने समय? *kya : kitne samay*

what's the time? कितने बजे हैं? *kitne baje hain*

what kind of? किस तरह का? *kis tarah kaa*

wheelchair व्हील चेयर *wheel chair*

when? कब? *kub*

where? कहाँ? *kahan*

where are you from? आप कहाँ से आए हैं? *aap kahan se aaye hain*

where is the? कहाँ है? *kahan hai*

where were you born? आप का जन्म कहाँ

हुआ था? *aapkaa janam kahan hua tha*

which? कौन सा? *kaun saa*

white सफेद *white*

wine मदिरा *madiraa*

who? कौन? *kaun*

whose? किसका? *kiskaa*

why? क्यों? *kyon*

wide चौड़ा *chaudaa*

wife पत्नी *patni*

WiFi वाईफाई *wifi*

wildlife वन जीवन *vun jeevan*

windbreaker विंडब्रेकर *windbreaker*

window खिड़की *khirkee;* **~ seat** खिड़की के पास वाली सीट *khirkee ke paas waali seat*

windscreen विंडस्क्रीन *windscreen*

windy, to be हवादार होना *hawadaar hona*

wine मदिरा *madiraa;* **~ list** मदिरा सूची *madiraa soochi*

winter जाड़ा *jaadaa*

wishes: best wishes शुभकामनाएं: *shubhkaamnaay*

with साथ *saath*

withdraw, to निकालना *nikaalnaa*

within में *mein*

without बिना *bina*

witness गवाह *gawah*

wood जंगल *jungle*

wool ऊन *oon*

work:~ for काम:~ के लिए काम *kaam: ke liye kaam*

it doesn't work यह काम नहीं करता *yeh kaam nahin kurta*

worse बदतर *budtur*

worst सबसे बुरा *sabse buraa*

wound घाव *ghaav*

write down, to लिखना *likhnaa*

wrong गलत *galat* **~ number** गलत नंबर *galat number;* **to be** ~ गलत होना *galat hona*

there's something wrong with के साथ कुछ गड़बड़ है *ke saath kuch gadbad hai*

X

X-ray एक्स रे *X-ray*

Y

yacht यॉट *yacht*

year साल *saal*

yellow पीला *peela*

yes हां *haan*

yesterday कल *kul*

yogurt दही *dahi*

you (formal) आप *aap* **(informal)** तुम *tum*

young जवान *jawaan*

your(s) *(pl.)* आपका *aapkaa (sing.)* आप लोगों का *aap logon kaa*

youth hostel यूथ हॉस्टल *youth hostel*

Z

zero शून्य *hunya*

zip(per) जिपर *zipper*

INDEX

Berlitz pocket guide

RAJASTHAN

First Edition 2019

Editors: Tom Fleming and Aimee White
Author: Gavin Thomas
Head of DTP and Pre-Press: Rebeka Davies
Managing Editor: Carine Tracanelli
Picture Editor: Aude Vauconsant
Cartography Update: Carte
Photography Credits: Alamy 88, 104; Getty
Images 17, 18, 21, 22, 40, 55, 91, 94, 100,
102; iStock 4TC, 4MC, 4ML, 4TL, 5T, 5TC,
5MC, 5M, 5MC, 5M, 6L, 6R, 7, 7R, 12, 14,
26, 30, 32, 34, 37, 42, 44, 47, 48, 49, 50, 51,
53, 56, 61, 64, 69, 70, 72, 75, 80, 82, 85, 86;
iStock 93, 97, 99, 109; Shutterstock 11, 29,
39, 58, 63, 67, 76, 79, 87, 96, 106
Cover Picture: Getty Images

Distribution
UK, Ireland and Europe: Apa Publications
(UK) Ltd; sales@insightguides.com
United States and Canada: Ingram
Publisher Services; ips@ingramcontent.com
Australia and New Zealand: Woodslane;
info@woodslane.com.au
Southeast Asia: Apa Publications (SN) Pte;
singaporeoffice@insightguides.com
Worldwide: Apa Publications (UK) Ltd;
sales@insightguides.com

**Special Sales, Content Licensing
and CoPublishing**
Insight Guides can be purchased in bulk
quantities at discounted prices. We can

create special editions, personalised
jackets and corporate imprints tailored to
your needs. sales@insightguides.com;
www.insightguides.biz

Contact us
Every effort has been made to provide
accurate information in this publication,
but changes are inevitable. The publisher
cannot be responsible for any resulting loss,
inconvenience or injury. We would appreciate
it if readers would call our attention to any
errors or outdated information. We also
welcome your suggestions; please contact
us at: berlitz@apaguide.co.uk
www.insightguides.com/berlitz